100 Interview Questions
Kubernetes

X.Y. Wang

Contents

1 Introduction   2

2 Basic   4

    2.1   What is Kubernetes and why is it important? . . .   4

    2.2   Describe the main components of a Kubernetes architecture. 6

    2.3   What is a Kubernetes Pod and why is it essential in a cluster? 7

    2.4   Explain the role of a Kubernetes Service. 9

    2.5   What are Labels and Selectors in Kubernetes? Why are they important? 11

    2.6   Describe the key differences between a Node and a Cluster in Kubernetes. 12

    2.7   What is a Namespace in Kubernetes and what are its use cases? 14

    2.8   Explain the function of a Kubelet in Kubernetes. . 15

    2.9   How does container orchestration work in Kubernetes? 17

2.10 What are the main advantages of using Kubernetes compared to other container orchestration platforms? 18

2.11 Describe the difference between a ReplicaSet and a Replication Controller in Kubernetes. 20

2.12 What is a DaemonSet in Kubernetes and when is it used? 22

2.13 Explain the purpose of the kubectl command-line tool. 24

2.14 Describe the role of a Kubernetes ConfigMap. . . . 25

2.15 What is a Kubernetes Secret and how does it differ from a ConfigMap? 27

2.16 What is a Kubernetes Deployment and why is it important? 29

2.17 How do you expose an application in a Kubernetes cluster using a Service? 31

2.18 Describe the key components of a Kubernetes manifest file. 33

2.19 What is Horizontal Pod Autoscaling (HPA) in Kubernetes and how does it work? 35

2.20 Explain the difference between a LoadBalancer and a NodePort service type in Kubernetes. 36

3 Intermediate   39

3.1 What is a Deployment in Kubernetes and how does it differ from a ReplicaSet? 39

3.2 Explain the difference between a ConfigMap and a Secret, and when you should use each. 42

3.3 Describe the process of rolling updates in Kubernetes and its advantages. 44

3.4   How does Kubernetes handle container resource
      management, such as CPU and memory limits?   . . 46

3.5   Explain the role of a Kubernetes Ingress and how
      it differs from a Service.   48

3.6   Describe the concept of Kubernetes init containers
      and their use cases.   49

3.7   What is a readiness probe and a liveness probe in
      Kubernetes, and why are they important?   51

3.8   How does Kubernetes handle storage using Persis-
      tent Volumes (PV) and Persistent Volume Claims
      (PVC)?   52

3.9   Explain the concept of affinity and anti-affinity rules
      in Kubernetes.   54

3.10 How do you monitor the health of a Kubernetes
      cluster and its components?   55

3.11 Describe the process of updating a running Kuber-
      netes application with zero downtime.   57

3.12 What is a StatefulSet in Kubernetes and when should
      you use it?   58

3.13 Explain the process of rolling back a Deployment
      in Kubernetes.   60

3.14 What are Kubernetes Jobs and CronJobs, and what
      are their primary use cases?   62

3.15 Describe the process of autoscaling in Kubernetes
      using the Horizontal Pod Autoscaler (HPA) and the
      Cluster Autoscaler.   64

3.16 How can you use Helm to manage application de-
      ployments in Kubernetes?   66

3.17 Explain the difference between imperative, declara-
      tive, and hybrid approaches in managing Kubernetes
      resources.   69

3.18 What are Taints and Tolerations in Kubernetes, and how do they help in scheduling Pods on Nodes? . . 70

3.19 Discuss the role of Kubernetes Custom Resource Definitions (CRDs). 72

3.20 Describe the process of securing container images in a Kubernetes environment. 73

4 Advanced **76**

4.1 Describe the Kubernetes control plane and its components, including the API server, etcd, controller manager, and scheduler. 76

4.2 Explain the role of the Kubernetes API server in the control plane. 77

4.3 What is a StatefulSet and how does it differ from a Deployment in managing stateful applications? . . . 78

4.4 Describe the process of setting up High Availability (HA) in a Kubernetes cluster. 80

4.5 Explain how Kubernetes handles persistent storage using Persistent Volumes (PV), Persistent Volume Claims (PVC), and Storage Classes. 81

4.6 What are Kubernetes Operators, and how do they extend the functionality of the platform? 83

4.7 Discuss the key security features in Kubernetes, such as Role-Based Access Control (RBAC), Network Policies, and Pod Security Policies (PSP). . . 85

4.8 Describe the Kubernetes networking model, including the role of the Container Network Interface (CNI) and the use of network plugins. 87

4.9 What are Custom Resource Definitions (CRDs) in Kubernetes, and how do they enable extensibility? . 89

4.10 Explain how Kubernetes handles container logging
      and monitoring, including the role of Prometheus,
      Grafana, and Fluentd. 91

4.11 Describe the process of setting up a private con-
      tainer registry and integrating it with a Kubernetes
      cluster. 93

4.12 Explain how Kubernetes manages container im-
      age security, including image scanning and using a
      trusted base image. 95

4.13 Discuss the role of service meshes, such as Istio
      or Linkerd, in a Kubernetes environment and their
      advantages. 97

4.14 Explain the concept of GitOps and how it can be
      applied to manage Kubernetes deployments. 99

4.15 What is a PodDisruptionBudget (PDB) in Kuber-
      netes and how does it help maintain high availability
      during cluster maintenance? 101

4.16 Describe the process of implementing network seg-
      mentation and isolation using Kubernetes Network
      Policies. 102

4.17 Explain how Kubernetes manages Secrets and Con-
      figMaps, and how they can be used to inject config-
      uration data into applications. 104

4.18 Discuss the role of admission controllers in Kuber-
      netes and how they enhance security. 106

4.19 Explain the process of setting up and configuring a
      Kubernetes cluster from scratch. 107

4.20 Describe the role of Kubernetes Custom Controllers
      and how they can be used to automate and extend
      cluster functionality. 109

5 Expert   112

5.1 Describe the Kubernetes scheduler's algorithm for placing Pods on Nodes, considering factors like resource requirements, affinity rules, and taints/tolerations. 112

5.2 Explain the role of etcd in Kubernetes and its importance in maintaining the cluster's state. 114

5.3 How do you configure and manage Role-Based Access Control (RBAC) for cluster resources in Kubernetes? 116

5.4 Discuss the process of setting up and managing multi-tenant Kubernetes clusters, including resource quotas and Namespace isolation. 118

5.5 Explain how Kubernetes handles container networking using different CNI plugins and their pros and cons. 120

5.6 Describe the process of migrating applications between Kubernetes clusters, including strategies for data migration and zero-downtime deployments. . . 122

5.7 Explain how to set up and configure a service mesh like Istio or Linkerd in a Kubernetes environment, and discuss its benefits and challenges. 124

5.8 How do you monitor and manage the performance of a Kubernetes cluster, including identifying bottlenecks and optimizing resource usage? 126

5.9 Describe the process of integrating Kubernetes with third-party services and tools like CI/CD pipelines, monitoring platforms, and external authentication providers. 128

5.10 Explain how to implement disaster recovery strategies in a Kubernetes cluster, including backup/restore, multi-cluster replication, and failover. 130

5.11 Discuss the role of the Kubernetes API Aggregation and its use cases in extending the Kubernetes API. 132

5.12 Describe the process of building custom Kubernetes Operators using tools like Operator SDK and Kube-builder. 134

5.13 Explain how to troubleshoot common issues in a Kubernetes environment, including networking, storage, and application-related problems. 136

5.14 How do you optimize the performance of a Kubernetes cluster in terms of resource usage, scaling, and resiliency? 138

5.15 Describe the process of securing a Kubernetes cluster at different levels, including the control plane, worker nodes, and container images. 140

5.16 Discuss the role of Kubernetes Federated Clusters and their use cases in multi-region and multi-cloud deployments. 142

5.17 Explain how to implement end-to-end encryption in a Kubernetes cluster, including securing data at rest and in transit. 144

5.18 Describe the process of setting up and managing autoscaling groups in Kubernetes, including Vertical Pod Autoscaler (VPA) and Cluster Autoscaler. . . . 145

5.19 How do you ensure data persistence and durability in a Kubernetes cluster, considering factors like node failures, application crashes, and data corruption? . 147

5.20 Discuss the future of Kubernetes and its ecosystem, including potential improvements, emerging technologies, and best practices. 149

6 Guru 151

6.1 Explain in detail how the Kubernetes scheduler works, considering factors like scoring, filtering, and prioritization of nodes for Pod placement. 151

6.2 Discuss the concept of Kubernetes Federation, its architecture, and use cases, including multi-cluster management and cross-cluster service discovery. . . 153

6.3 Describe strategies for backing up and restoring a Kubernetes cluster, including etcd snapshots, Persistent Volume (PV) backups, and restoring API objects. 155

6.4 How do you implement advanced security measures in a Kubernetes cluster, such as encryption at rest, mutual TLS authentication, and image signing? . . 157

6.5 Explain the process of developing and deploying custom Kubernetes controllers, including their design patterns, lifecycle management, and integration with the cluster. 159

6.6 Discuss the role of service meshes in complex Kubernetes environments, including traffic management, security, and observability features, and compare different service mesh solutions. 161

6.7 Describe strategies for optimizing the performance of a Kubernetes cluster, including cluster autoscaling, optimizing resource usage, and implementing advanced Pod placement. 162

6.8 How do you manage and monitor large-scale, multi-cluster Kubernetes environments, including centralized logging, observability, and alerting? 164

6.9 Discuss the challenges and best practices in implementing multi-cloud and hybrid cloud Kubernetes deployments, including networking, storage, and resource management. 165

6.10 Explain the process of setting up and managing Kubernetes clusters on edge devices and IoT environments, and discuss the challenges and benefits of edge computing with Kubernetes. 167

6.11   Describe the role of Custom Resource Definitions
        (CRDs) and their controllers in implementing domain-
        specific extensions to Kubernetes. 169

6.12   How do you implement GitOps workflows in a Ku-
        bernetes environment, including versioning, rollbacks,
        and integration with CI/CD pipelines? 170

6.13   Discuss the process of container runtime interface
        (CRI) implementation in Kubernetes and compare
        different container runtime options. 172

6.14   Explain the role of Kubernetes Admission Web-
        hooks, their types (Validating and Mutating), and
        how they can be used to implement custom valida-
        tion and mutation logic. 173

6.15   Describe advanced networking concepts in Kuber-
        netes, such as network policies, ingress controllers,
        and service meshes, and discuss their impact on clus-
        ter performance and security. 175

6.16   Discuss strategies for implementing and enforcing
        compliance and governance policies in a Kubernetes
        environment, including cluster hardening, policy en-
        gines, and auditing. 177

6.17   Explain the process of integrating Kubernetes with
        external storage systems and databases, consider-
        ing factors like data consistency, latency, and back-
        up/restore strategies. 178

6.18   How do you manage cluster upgrades and versioning
        in a Kubernetes environment, including best prac-
        tices for minimizing downtime and ensuring back-
        ward compatibility? 180

6.19   Discuss the role of machine learning and artificial
        intelligence in optimizing Kubernetes cluster man-
        agement, including workload placement, autoscal-
        ing, and anomaly detection. 181

6.20 Describe the challenges and opportunities in the evolution of the Kubernetes ecosystem, including emerging technologies, open-source projects, and community-driven initiatives. 183

Chapter 1

Introduction

Welcome to "100 Interview Questions - Kubernetes", a comprehensive guide designed to help you prepare for Kubernetes-related interviews or simply deepen your understanding of this powerful container orchestration platform. This book is organized into four sections, each targeting a different level of expertise - from basic to guru - so you can find the right questions and answers to suit your needs.

Kubernetes is an open-source container orchestration platform that automates the deployment, scaling, and management of containerized applications. Developed by Google and later donated to the Cloud Native Computing Foundation (CNCF), Kubernetes has grown into one of the most popular and widely adopted container orchestration platforms in the world. With the increasing popularity of microservices architectures and cloud-native application development, Kubernetes has become an essential tool for developers and operations teams alike.

As Kubernetes continues to gain traction, the demand for professionals with Kubernetes knowledge and experience is also on the rise. Whether you're an aspiring DevOps engineer, a cloud architect, or a software developer, understanding Kubernetes concepts and best practices can give you a competitive edge in the job market.

This book is structured to provide you with a comprehensive set of interview questions and answers across various levels of complexity. Starting with basic questions, you will first build a foundation in Kubernetes fundamentals. As you progress through the book, the questions will become increasingly more challenging, covering intermediate and advanced topics. Finally, you will encounter expert and guru-level questions that test your deep understanding of Kubernetes and its ecosystem.

Each question is accompanied by a thorough explanation to ensure that you not only know the right answer but also understand the underlying concepts. As you work through the questions and answers, you will develop a strong understanding of Kubernetes, its architecture, and its core components. Furthermore, you will learn how to deploy and manage applications on Kubernetes, troubleshoot common issues, and optimize cluster performance.

In addition to preparing you for Kubernetes-related interviews, this book can serve as a handy reference guide for professionals already working with Kubernetes. By reviewing the questions and answers, you can refresh your knowledge, learn new features, and stay up to date with the latest best practices in the ever-evolving Kubernetes ecosystem.

So, whether you're preparing for an interview or simply seeking to improve your Kubernetes skills, "100 Interview Questions - Kubernetes" is here to help you on your journey. Grab your favorite beverage, sit back, and let's dive into the fascinating world of Kubernetes!

Chapter 2

Basic

2.1 What is Kubernetes and why is it important?

Kubernetes is an open-source container orchestration platform that automates the deployment, scaling, and management of containerized applications. It provides a powerful and flexible platform for running and managing distributed applications across a cluster of servers.

With Kubernetes, developers can focus on writing code while allowing administrators to manage infrastructure, networking, and storage resources. Kubernetes provides the following benefits:

Scalability: Kubernetes makes it easy to scale applications up or down based on demand. It can automatically adjust the number of containers running based on the application workload, ensuring that the application is always available and responsive.

Availability: Kubernetes provides automated failover and self-healing capabilities, ensuring that applications are always available even if a container or node fails.

Flexibility: Kubernetes allows developers to use any programming language, framework, or tool to build their applications. It also supports a wide range of container runtimes, such as Docker and containerd.

Portability: Kubernetes provides a consistent and portable platform for running applications across different environments, such as on-premises, public cloud, or hybrid cloud.

Here's an example of deploying a simple application to Kubernetes using a Deployment resource:

```
apiVersion: apps/v1
kind: Deployment
metadata:
  name: my-app
spec:
  replicas: 3
  selector:
    matchLabels:
      app: my-app
  template:
    metadata:
      labels:
        app: my-app
    spec:
      containers:
      - name: my-app
        image: my-image:latest
        ports:
        - containerPort: 8080
```

In this example, we define a Deployment resource called my-app that will run three replicas of a container running the my-image image on port 8080. The selector field specifies how the replicas are selected, and the template field specifies the configuration for the Pods that will be created.

We can deploy this resource to Kubernetes using the following command:

```
kubectl apply -f deployment.yaml
```

This command tells Kubernetes to create or update the resources defined in the deployment.yaml file.

In conclusion, Kubernetes is important because it provides a powerful and flexible platform for running and managing containerized applications. It enables developers to focus on writing code while allowing administrators to manage infrastructure resources. Kubernetes provides scalability, availability, flexibility, and portability, making it an essential tool for building and deploying modern applications.

2.2 Describe the main components of a Kubernetes architecture.

The main components of a Kubernetes architecture are as follows:

Control Plane: The Control Plane is responsible for managing the cluster state, scheduling applications, and managing the overall health of the cluster. It consists of the following components: etcd: A distributed key-value store that stores the configuration data for the cluster.

kube-apiserver: The central control plane component that exposes the Kubernetes API, which is used to manage the cluster state.

kube-scheduler: The component responsible for scheduling applications onto Nodes based on available resources and application requirements.

kube-controller-manager: The component responsible for managing the state of the cluster and performing tasks such as scaling, updating, and deleting resources.

Nodes: Nodes are the worker machines that run containerized applications. They are responsible for running Pods and reporting their status to the Control Plane. Each Node runs the following components:

kubelet: The component responsible for communicating with the Control Plane and managing the Pods and containers running on the Node.

kube-proxy: The component responsible for routing network traffic to the appropriate Pods and Services.

Networking: Kubernetes provides a flexible networking model that allows Pods to communicate with each other and with external network resources. Kubernetes uses a flat networking model where each Pod has its own IP address, and Services provide a stable IP address and DNS name for a set of Pods.

Here's an example of using kubectl to view the components running in a Kubernetes cluster:

```
kubectl get componentstatuses
```

This command shows the status of the various Kubernetes components, including the etcd nodes, kube-apiserver, kube-scheduler, and kube-controller-manager.

Here's an example of using kubectl to view the Nodes in a Kubernetes cluster:

```
kubectl get nodes
```

This command shows the Nodes in the cluster, including their hostname, IP address, and status.

Here's an example of using kubectl to view the Pods running on a Node:

```
kubectl get pods --all-namespaces -o wide
```

This command shows the Pods running on all Nodes in the cluster, along with their namespace, name, IP address, and status.

In conclusion, Kubernetes architecture consists of a Control Plane that manages the cluster state, Nodes that run containerized applications, and a flexible networking model that enables communication between Pods and external network resources. Understanding the architecture of Kubernetes is essential for building and deploying containerized applications on a Kubernetes cluster.

2.3 What is a Kubernetes Pod and why is it essential in a cluster?

A Kubernetes Pod is the smallest deployable unit in the Kubernetes system. It represents a single instance of a running process in a cluster. A Pod consists of one or more containers, and all containers within a Pod share the same network namespace and can communicate with each other using localhost. Pods are ephemeral and can be created, scaled, and destroyed dynamically based on the application requirements.

Pods are essential in a Kubernetes cluster because they provide a way to run and manage containerized applications. Pods provide the following benefits:

Encapsulation: Pods encapsulate the application code and dependencies, making it easy to package, deploy, and manage containerized applications.

Resource sharing: Containers within a Pod share the same network namespace and can communicate with each other using localhost. They also share the same filesystem, which allows them to share files and resources.

Scalability: Pods can be scaled up or down based on application demand. Kubernetes can create or destroy Pods dynamically to ensure that the application is always available and responsive.

Health monitoring: Kubernetes monitors the health of Pods and can automatically restart them if they fail. This ensures that the application is always available and responsive.

Here's an example of defining a Pod in Kubernetes:

```
apiVersion: v1
kind: Pod
metadata:
  name: my-pod
spec:
  containers:
  - name: my-container
    image: my-image:latest
    ports:
    - containerPort: 8080
```

In this example, we define a Pod resource called my-pod that will run a single container using the my-image image on port 8080. The spec field specifies the configuration for the container.

We can deploy this resource to Kubernetes using the following command:

```
kubectl apply -f pod.yaml
```

This command tells Kubernetes to create or update the Pod resource defined in the pod.yaml file.

Here's an example of using kubectl to view the Pods running in a
Kubernetes cluster:

```
kubectl get pods
```

This command shows the Pods running in the cluster, including
their name, status, and IP address.

In conclusion, Kubernetes Pods are essential in a Kubernetes cluster because they provide a way to run and manage containerized
applications. Pods encapsulate the application code and dependencies, share resources, enable scalability, and support health monitoring. Understanding Pods is essential for building and deploying
containerized applications on a Kubernetes cluster.

2.4   Explain the role of a Kubernetes Service.

A Kubernetes Service is an abstraction that defines a logical set of
Pods and a policy by which to access them. Services enable communication between Pods and external network endpoints, such as
load balancers, other Services, and external clients. A Service provides a stable IP address and DNS name for a set of Pods, even as
they are created, scaled, and destroyed over time.

The role of a Kubernetes Service is to provide a way to expose the
Pods running in a cluster to other components within or outside
the cluster. Services provide the following benefits:

Load balancing: Services can distribute network traffic across multiple Pods, providing load balancing for the application.

Service discovery: Services provide a stable IP address and DNS
name for a set of Pods, making it easy for other components within
or outside the cluster to discover and access the application.

Health checking: Services can monitor the health of the underlying
Pods and automatically route traffic away from unhealthy Pods.

IP address management: Services provide a way to manage the IP
addresses assigned to Pods, ensuring that applications can be ac-

cessed consistently even as Pods are created, scaled, and destroyed over time.

Here's an example of defining a Service in Kubernetes:

```
apiVersion: v1
kind: Service
metadata:
  name: my-service
spec:
  selector:
    app: my-app
  ports:
  - name: http
    port: 80
    targetPort: 8080
  type: LoadBalancer
```

In this example, we define a Service resource called my-service that will route traffic to Pods with the label app: my-app. The ports field specifies that incoming traffic on port 80 should be routed to the container port 8080. The type field specifies that the Service should be exposed externally as a load balancer.

We can deploy this resource to Kubernetes using the following command:

```
kubectl apply -f service.yaml
```

This command tells Kubernetes to create or update the Service resource defined in the service.yaml file.

Here's an example of using kubectl to view the Services running in a Kubernetes cluster:

```
kubectl get services
```

This command shows the Services running in the cluster, including their name, type, cluster IP address, external IP address, and port mappings.

In conclusion, Kubernetes Services provide a way to expose the Pods running in a cluster to other components within or outside the cluster. Services enable load balancing, service discovery, health checking, and IP address management, making it easy to build and deploy scalable and resilient applications on a Kubernetes cluster.

2.5 What are Labels and Selectors in Kubernetes? Why are they important?

Labels and Selectors are two key concepts in Kubernetes that provide a way to organize and manage resources within a cluster.

Labels are key-value pairs that can be attached to Kubernetes resources, such as Pods, Services, and Deployments. Labels are used to mark resources with metadata that can be used to identify and group them. Labels are flexible and can be used for a variety of purposes, such as identifying the environment, version, or owner of a resource.

Selectors are used to select a subset of resources based on their labels. Selectors are defined using label expressions, which are used to match labels on resources. Selectors enable resources to be grouped and selected based on their metadata, allowing for fine-grained control over how resources are managed.

Labels and Selectors are important in Kubernetes because they provide a way to organize and manage resources within a cluster. They enable the following use cases:

Grouping resources: Labels provide a way to group related resources together, making it easy to manage and organize them. For example, you could use labels to group all of the Pods and Services related to a particular application.

Selecting resources: Selectors provide a way to select a subset of resources based on their metadata. This allows you to target specific resources for management tasks, such as scaling, updating, or deleting.

Routing traffic: Services use selectors to route traffic to the appropriate Pods. This allows Services to distribute traffic across multiple Pods, providing load balancing for the application.

Here's an example of using labels and selectors in Kubernetes:

```
apiVersion: v1
kind: Pod
metadata:
```

```
   name: my-pod
   labels:
     app: my-app
     version: v1
spec:
   containers:
   - name: my-container
     image: my-image:latest
     ports:
     - containerPort: 8080
```

In this example, we define a Pod resource called my-pod with two labels: app: my-app and version: v1. We can use these labels to group and select the Pod for management tasks.

Here's an example of using a selector to select resources based on their labels:

```
kubectl get pods -l app=my-app
```

This command selects all Pods with the label app: my-app and displays information about them.

In conclusion, Labels and Selectors are important in Kubernetes because they provide a way to organize and manage resources within a cluster. They enable grouping, selecting, and routing of resources based on their metadata, making it easy to manage and scale applications on a Kubernetes cluster.

2.6 Describe the key differences between a Node and a Cluster in Kubernetes.

In Kubernetes, a Node and a Cluster are two different concepts that serve different purposes.

A Node is a worker machine in Kubernetes that runs containerized applications. Each Node runs one or more Pods, and Pods are the smallest deployable units in Kubernetes. Nodes provide the computing resources needed to run applications, such as CPU, memory, and storage. Nodes are managed by the Control Plane, which schedules Pods onto Nodes based on available resources and application requirements.

A Cluster, on the other hand, is a collection of Nodes that work together to run containerized applications. A Cluster provides a way to manage the state of the cluster, schedule applications, and manage networking and storage resources. A Cluster consists of one or more Nodes, and applications can be deployed and scaled across multiple Nodes in the Cluster.

The key differences between a Node and a Cluster in Kubernetes are as follows:

Scope: Nodes are the smallest deployable units in Kubernetes and are used to run containerized applications. Clusters, on the other hand, provide a way to manage multiple Nodes and the resources needed to run applications across them.

Management: Nodes are managed by the Control Plane, which schedules Pods onto Nodes based on available resources and application requirements. Clusters are managed by the administrator, who is responsible for deploying and managing the infrastructure, networking, and storage resources needed to support the applications running in the Cluster.

Resources: Nodes provide the computing resources needed to run containerized applications, such as CPU, memory, and storage. Clusters provide a way to manage and distribute those resources across multiple Nodes.

Here's an example of using kubectl to view the Nodes in a Kubernetes cluster:

```
kubectl get nodes
```

This command shows the Nodes in the cluster, including their hostname, IP address, and status.

Here's an example of using kubectl to view the Pods running on a Node:

```
kubectl get pods --all-namespaces -o wide
```

This command shows the Pods running on all Nodes in the cluster, along with their namespace, name, IP address, and status.

In conclusion, Nodes and Clusters are two different concepts in Kubernetes that serve different purposes. Nodes provide the computing resources needed to run containerized applications, while Clusters provide a way to manage and distribute those resources across multiple Nodes. Understanding the differences between Nodes and Clusters is essential for building and deploying containerized applications on a Kubernetes cluster.

2.7 What is a Namespace in Kubernetes and what are its use cases?

In Kubernetes, a Namespace is a way to organize and isolate resources within a cluster. Namespaces provide a scope for names and prevent naming conflicts between multiple teams or applications. They also enable resource sharing and resource quotas within a cluster.

A Namespace is a logical space within a Kubernetes cluster that provides a way to group and manage resources. Each Namespace has its own set of resources, including Pods, Services, Deployments, ConfigMaps, and Secrets. Namespaces provide the following benefits:

Resource isolation: Namespaces provide a way to isolate resources and prevent naming conflicts between multiple teams or applications. Each Namespace has its own set of resources and can be managed independently of other Namespaces.

Resource sharing: Namespaces enable resource sharing within a cluster. Resources can be shared between different applications or teams by creating them in a shared Namespace.

Resource quotas: Namespaces provide a way to enforce resource quotas within a cluster. Quotas can be set for CPU, memory, and storage resources to prevent overuse and ensure fair resource allocation.

Access control: Namespaces provide a way to control access to resources within a cluster. Roles and RoleBindings can be used to grant or deny access to resources within a Namespace.

Here's an example of using kubectl to create a Namespace in Kubernetes:

```
kubectl create namespace my-namespace
```

This command creates a Namespace called my-namespace in the Kubernetes cluster.

Here's an example of using kubectl to deploy resources in a specific Namespace:

```
kubectl apply -f my-resource.yaml -n my-namespace
```

This command deploys a resource defined in the my-resource.yaml file to the Namespace my-namespace.

Here's an example of using kubectl to view the Namespaces in a Kubernetes cluster:

```
kubectl get namespaces
```

This command shows the Namespaces in the cluster, including their name, status, and creation timestamp.

In conclusion, Namespaces in Kubernetes provide a way to organize and isolate resources within a cluster. They enable resource sharing, resource quotas, and access control within a cluster, making it easy to manage and scale complex applications on a Kubernetes cluster. Understanding the use cases for Namespaces is essential for building and deploying containerized applications on a Kubernetes cluster.

2.8 Explain the function of a Kubelet in Kubernetes.

A Kubelet is an agent that runs on each Node in a Kubernetes cluster. The Kubelet is responsible for managing the lifecycle of Pods running on the Node, ensuring that the Pods are running and healthy.

The Kubelet is responsible for the following tasks:

Pod creation and deletion: The Kubelet creates and deletes Pods on the Node based on the Pod specification provided by the API server.

Pod health monitoring: The Kubelet monitors the health of the Pods running on the Node and reports their status to the API server. If a Pod fails, the Kubelet can automatically restart the Pod or take other actions to remediate the issue.

Node resource management: The Kubelet monitors the Node's available resources, such as CPU, memory, and storage, and ensures that Pods do not consume more resources than are available.

Pod networking: The Kubelet ensures that the Pods on the Node are properly networked, and that they can communicate with other Pods and Services in the cluster.

Here's an example of using kubectl to view the Kubelets running in a Kubernetes cluster:

```
kubectl get kubelets
```

This command shows the Kubelets running on each Node in the cluster, including their hostname, IP address, and status.

Here's an example of using kubectl to view the Pods running on a specific Node:

```
kubectl get pods --all-namespaces -o wide --node-name=node-1
```

This command shows the Pods running on the Node with the name node-1, including their namespace, name, IP address, and status.

In conclusion, a Kubelet is an agent that runs on each Node in a Kubernetes cluster and is responsible for managing the lifecycle of Pods running on the Node. The Kubelet performs tasks such as Pod creation and deletion, Pod health monitoring, Node resource management, and Pod networking. Understanding the function of the Kubelet is essential for building and deploying containerized applications on a Kubernetes cluster.

2.9 How does container orchestration work in Kubernetes?

Container orchestration in Kubernetes involves the management of containerized applications across a cluster of machines. Kubernetes provides a set of features that enable container orchestration, including workload management, service discovery, load balancing, and scaling.

Here's how container orchestration works in Kubernetes:

Workload Management: Kubernetes manages containerized applications as workloads, which can be deployed as Pods or as higher-level abstractions such as Deployments or StatefulSets. Workloads define the desired state of the application and Kubernetes ensures that the actual state matches the desired state.

Service Discovery: Kubernetes provides a way to discover services running within a cluster. Services are created to define a logical set of Pods and a policy by which to access them. They provide a stable IP address and DNS name for a set of Pods, even as they are created, scaled, and destroyed over time.

Load Balancing: Kubernetes can distribute network traffic across multiple Pods, providing load balancing for the application. This is achieved through the use of Services and Ingresses, which provide a single point of entry for external traffic and route traffic to the appropriate Pods.

Scaling: Kubernetes can automatically scale applications up or down based on resource utilization or other factors. This is achieved through the use of Controllers, which manage the lifecycle of Pods and ensure that the desired number of Pods are running at all times.

Here's an example of using kubectl to create a Deployment in Kubernetes:

```
apiVersion: apps/v1
kind: Deployment
metadata:
  name: my-deployment
spec:
  replicas: 3
  selector:
```

```
    matchLabels:
        app: my-app
    template:
        metadata:
            labels:
                app: my-app
        spec:
            containers:
            - name: my-container
              image: my-image:latest
              ports:
              - containerPort: 8080
```

This deployment will ensure that three Pods running the container image my-image:latest are running at all times. The Pods will be managed by the Deployment, and if any of the Pods fail, the Deployment will automatically create a new Pod to replace it.

Here's an example of using kubectl to scale a Deployment in Kubernetes:

```
kubectl scale deployment my-deployment --replicas=5
```

This command will increase the number of replicas for the Deployment my-deployment to 5, ensuring that five Pods are running at all times.

In conclusion, container orchestration in Kubernetes involves the management of containerized applications across a cluster of machines. Kubernetes provides a set of features that enable workload management, service discovery, load balancing, and scaling, making it easy to deploy and manage containerized applications on a Kubernetes cluster. Understanding how container orchestration works in Kubernetes is essential for building and deploying scalable and resilient applications on a Kubernetes cluster.

2.10 What are the main advantages of using Kubernetes compared to other container orchestration platforms?

Kubernetes is a widely used container orchestration platform that offers many advantages compared to other container orchestration platforms. Here are some of the main advantages of using Kubernetes:

Portability: Kubernetes is highly portable, meaning that it can be deployed on a variety of cloud providers, on-premises data centers, and even on personal computers. This makes it easy to move workloads between different environments, without having to worry about the underlying infrastructure.

Scalability: Kubernetes makes it easy to scale containerized applications up or down based on demand. This is achieved through the use of Controllers, which manage the lifecycle of Pods and ensure that the desired number of replicas are running at all times.

Resilience: Kubernetes is highly resilient, meaning that it can recover quickly from failures. This is achieved through the use of features such as self-healing and automatic rolling updates, which ensure that the application remains available even in the event of failures.

Flexibility: Kubernetes provides a flexible platform for deploying containerized applications, supporting a wide range of container runtimes and container images. This makes it easy to deploy applications built on different stacks and technologies.

Community: Kubernetes has a large and active community of developers, contributors, and users. This means that there is a wealth of resources available for learning and troubleshooting, as well as a large ecosystem of tools and plugins that can be used with Kubernetes.

Here's an example of using kubectl to view the status of a Kubernetes cluster:

```
kubectl cluster-info
```

This command displays information about the Kubernetes cluster, including the master and worker nodes, as well as the version of Kubernetes that is running.

Here's an example of using kubectl to deploy an application in Kubernetes:

```
kubectl create deployment my-app --image=my-image:latest
```

This command creates a deployment called my-app that runs the container image my-image:latest. The deployment will ensure that the desired number of replicas are running at all times, and will automatically replace any failed Pods.

In conclusion, Kubernetes offers many advantages compared to other container orchestration platforms. It is highly portable, scalable, resilient, flexible, and has a large and active community. These features make it an ideal platform for deploying and managing containerized applications at scale.

2.11   Describe the difference between a ReplicaSet and a Replication Controller in Kubernetes.

In Kubernetes, both ReplicaSets and Replication Controllers are used to ensure that a specified number of Pod replicas are running at all times. However, there are some key differences between these two objects.

A ReplicaSet is a newer and more advanced version of the Replication Controller. It provides more powerful and flexible options for managing the lifecycle of Pods.

Here are some of the key differences between a ReplicaSet and a Replication Controller:

Label selector matching: ReplicaSets use set-based selector matching, which is more powerful than the equality-based matching used by Replication Controllers. This means that ReplicaSets can match a wider range of labels and label expressions.

Rollout updates: ReplicaSets support rolling updates, which allows for gradual updates of Pods, rather than all-at-once updates. This makes it easier to deploy new versions of an application without downtime.

Scaling behavior: ReplicaSets have more granular scaling behavior, which allows for scaling based on a wider range of metrics, such as CPU and memory usage. This allows for more efficient resource utilization.

Object name: The name of a ReplicaSet object is different from a Replication Controller object. This means that you cannot perform a direct update from a Replication Controller to a ReplicaSet.

Here's an example of using kubectl to create a Replication Controller in Kubernetes:

```
apiVersion: v1
kind: ReplicationController
metadata:
  name: my-replication-controller
spec:
  replicas: 3
  selector:
    app: my-app
  template:
    metadata:
      labels:
        app: my-app
    spec:
      containers:
      - name: my-container
        image: my-image:latest
        ports:
        - containerPort: 8080
```

This replication controller will ensure that three replicas of the Pod running the container image my-image:latest are running at all times. The Pod will be managed by the replication controller, and if any of the Pods fail, the replication controller will automatically create a new Pod to replace it.

Here's an example of using kubectl to create a ReplicaSet in Kubernetes:

```
apiVersion: apps/v1
kind: ReplicaSet
metadata:
  name: my-replicaset
spec:
  replicas: 3
  selector:
    matchLabels:
      app: my-app
  template:
    metadata:
      labels:
        app: my-app
    spec:
      containers:
      - name: my-container
        image: my-image:latest
        ports:
        - containerPort: 8080
```

This ReplicaSet will also ensure that three replicas of the Pod running the container image my-image:latest are running at all times. The Pod will be managed by the ReplicaSet, and if any of the Pods fail, the ReplicaSet will automatically create a new Pod to replace it.

In conclusion, ReplicaSets and Replication Controllers are used to ensure that a specified number of Pod replicas are running at all times. However, ReplicaSets are a newer and more advanced version of the Replication Controller, providing more powerful and flexible options for managing the lifecycle of Pods. Understanding the differences between ReplicaSets and Replication Controllers is important for managing containerized applications in a Kubernetes cluster.

2.12   What is a DaemonSet in Kubernetes and when is it used?

A DaemonSet in Kubernetes is a type of workload that ensures that a copy of a Pod is running on each Node in the cluster. DaemonSets are typically used for system-level or infrastructure-related tasks, such as monitoring, logging, or networking.

Here are some use cases for DaemonSets in Kubernetes:

Node-level monitoring: DaemonSets can be used to deploy monitoring agents on each Node in the cluster, allowing for node-level monitoring of system metrics such as CPU usage, memory usage, and disk space.

Log collection: DaemonSets can be used to collect logs from each Node in the cluster, allowing for centralized logging and analysis of application logs.

Networking: DaemonSets can be used to deploy networking agents, such as proxies or load balancers, on each Node in the cluster, allowing for efficient and scalable networking.

Security: DaemonSets can be used to deploy security agents, such as firewalls or intrusion detection systems, on each Node in the cluster, allowing for enhanced security and threat detection.

Here's an example of using kubectl to create a DaemonSet in Kubernetes:

```
apiVersion: apps/v1
kind: DaemonSet
metadata:
  name: my-daemonset
spec:
  selector:
    matchLabels:
      app: my-app
  template:
    metadata:
      labels:
        app: my-app
    spec:
      containers:
      - name: my-container
        image: my-image:latest
        ports:
        - containerPort: 8080
```

This DaemonSet will ensure that a copy of the Pod running the container image my-image:latest is running on each Node in the cluster. The Pod will be managed by the DaemonSet, and if a new Node is added to the cluster, the DaemonSet will automatically create a new Pod to run on that Node.

Here's an example of using kubectl to view the DaemonSets running in a Kubernetes cluster:

```
kubectl get daemonsets
```

This command shows the DaemonSets running in the cluster, including their name, desired number of replicas, and current status.

In conclusion, a DaemonSet in Kubernetes is a type of workload that ensures that a copy of a Pod is running on each Node in the cluster. DaemonSets are typically used for system-level or infrastructure-related tasks, such as monitoring, logging, or networking. Understanding the use cases for DaemonSets in Kubernetes is important for deploying and managing containerized applications in a Kubernetes cluster.

2.13 Explain the purpose of the kubectl command-line tool.

The kubectl command-line tool is the primary interface for managing Kubernetes clusters. It is a command-line tool that allows users to interact with the Kubernetes API server, and perform various tasks such as deploying and scaling applications, managing Pods, and viewing cluster information.

Here are some of the key features of the kubectl command-line tool:

Cluster Management: kubectl allows users to manage Kubernetes clusters, including creating and deleting clusters, viewing cluster information, and managing authentication and access control.

Resource Management: kubectl allows users to manage Kubernetes resources, including creating, deleting, updating, and scaling Pods, Deployments, Services, and other Kubernetes objects.

Debugging and Troubleshooting: kubectl provides various commands for debugging and troubleshooting Kubernetes clusters, including viewing logs, describing resources, and inspecting network connections.

Customization and Extension: kubectl can be extended with custom plugins and scripts, allowing users to automate common tasks and add custom functionality.

Here are some example commands for using kubectl to manage a Kubernetes cluster:

Deploy an application:

```
kubectl create deployment my-app --image=my-image:latest
```

This command creates a deployment called my-app that runs the container image my-image:latest.

Scale a Deployment:

```
kubectl scale deployment my-app --replicas=3
```

This command increases the number of replicas for the Deployment my-app to 3.

View Pod logs:

```
kubectl logs my-pod
```

This command shows the logs for the Pod my-pod.

Describe a Kubernetes object:

```
kubectl describe deployment my-app
```

This command shows detailed information about the Deployment my-app, including its current status, Pod template, and associated resources.

In conclusion, the kubectl command-line tool is the primary interface for managing Kubernetes clusters. It provides various commands for managing cluster resources, debugging and troubleshooting, and customizing and extending the tool. Understanding how to use kubectl is essential for managing containerized applications in a Kubernetes cluster.

2.14   Describe the role of a Kubernetes ConfigMap.

A ConfigMap in Kubernetes is a way to store configuration data as key-value pairs that can be used by containers in a Pod. ConfigMaps are used to separate configuration data from the application code, making it easier to manage and update configuration data without having to rebuild or redeploy the application.

Here are some common use cases for ConfigMaps in Kubernetes:

Application configuration: ConfigMaps can be used to store application configuration data such as database connection strings, API keys, and other environment-specific settings.

Environment variables: ConfigMaps can be used to set environment variables that are used by containers in a Pod. This allows for greater flexibility in configuring containers and makes it easier to change environment variables without having to rebuild or redeploy the container image.

Command-line arguments: ConfigMaps can be used to set command-line arguments for containers in a Pod. This allows for greater flexibility in configuring containers and makes it easier to change command-line arguments without having to rebuild or redeploy the container image.

Here's an example of using kubectl to create a ConfigMap in Kubernetes:

```
apiVersion: v1
kind: ConfigMap
metadata:
  name: my-config
data:
  database.url: "http://my-database.com"
  api.key: "my-api-key"
```

This ConfigMap contains two key-value pairs: database.url with a value of http://my-database.com, and api.key with a value of my-api-key. These values can be accessed by containers in a Pod using environment variables or command-line arguments.

Here's an example of using kubectl to set environment variables using a ConfigMap:

```
apiVersion: v1
kind: Pod
metadata:
  name: my-pod
spec:
  containers:
  - name: my-container
    image: my-image:latest
    env:
    - name: DATABASE\_URL
      valueFrom:
        configMapKeyRef:
          name: my-config
          key: database.url
```

This Pod contains a container called my-container that uses the image my-image:latest. The env field sets the environment variable DATABASE_URL to the value of the database.url key in the ConfigMap my-config.

Here's an example of using kubectl to set command-line arguments using a ConfigMap:

```
apiVersion: v1
kind: Pod
metadata:
  name: my-pod
```

```
spec:
  containers:
  - name: my-container
    image: my-image:latest
    command: ["/bin/my-app"]
    args: ["--api-key=\$(API\_KEY)"]
    env:
    - name: API\_KEY
      valueFrom:
        configMapKeyRef:
          name: my-config
          key: api.key
```

This Pod contains a container called my-container that uses the image my-image:latest. The command and args fields specify the command-line arguments for the container, with the –api-key argument set to the value of the api.key key in the ConfigMap my-config.

In conclusion, a ConfigMap in Kubernetes is a way to store configuration data as key-value pairs that can be used by containers in a Pod. ConfigMaps are used to separate configuration data from the application code, making it easier to manage and update configuration data without having to rebuild or redeploy the application. Understanding the role of ConfigMaps in Kubernetes is important for managing and configuring containerized applications in a Kubernetes cluster.

2.15   What is a Kubernetes Secret and how does it differ from a ConfigMap?

A Secret in Kubernetes is a way to store sensitive data such as passwords, tokens, and encryption keys as key-value pairs that can be used by containers in a Pod. Secrets are similar to ConfigMaps in that they allow for separation of sensitive data from application code, but Secrets are specifically designed to store confidential information that should be kept secure.

Here are some use cases for Secrets in Kubernetes:

Authentication: Secrets can be used to store authentication credentials such as passwords and access tokens for external services.

Encryption: Secrets can be used to store encryption keys and other sensitive data required for data encryption.

Application secrets: Secrets can be used to store application-specific secrets such as API keys and other sensitive data.

Here's an example of using kubectl to create a Secret in Kubernetes:

```
apiVersion: v1
kind: Secret
metadata:
  name: my-secret
type: Opaque
data:
  username: dXNlcm5hbWU=
  password: cGFzc3dvcmQ=
```

This Secret contains two key-value pairs: username with a base64-encoded value of username, and password with a base64-encoded value of password. These values can be accessed by containers in a Pod using environment variables or command-line arguments.

Here's an example of using kubectl to set environment variables using a Secret:

```
apiVersion: v1
kind: Pod
metadata:
  name: my-pod
spec:
  containers:
  - name: my-container
    image: my-image:latest
    env:
    - name: USERNAME
      valueFrom:
        secretKeyRef:
          name: my-secret
          key: username
    - name: PASSWORD
      valueFrom:
        secretKeyRef:
          name: my-secret
          key: password
```

This Pod contains a container called my-container that uses the image my-image:latest. The env field sets the environment variables USERNAME and PASSWORD to the values of the username and password keys in the Secret my-secret.

The main difference between a ConfigMap and a Secret in Kubernetes is that Secrets are specifically designed to store sensitive data that should be kept secure. Secrets are stored in a way that prevents unauthorized access, and can be encrypted at rest to provide an additional layer of security. ConfigMaps, on the other hand, are used to store configuration data that is not necessarily sensitive.

In conclusion, a Secret in Kubernetes is a way to store sensitive data such as passwords, tokens, and encryption keys as key-value pairs that can be used by containers in a Pod. Secrets are similar to ConfigMaps in that they allow for separation of sensitive data from application code, but Secrets are specifically designed to store confidential information that should be kept secure. Understanding the differences between ConfigMaps and Secrets in Kubernetes is important for managing and securing containerized applications in a Kubernetes cluster.

2.16 What is a Kubernetes Deployment and why is it important?

A Deployment in Kubernetes is a higher-level abstraction that is used to manage the lifecycle of Pods. Deployments are used to ensure that a specified number of replica Pods are running at all times, and can be used to manage rolling updates and rollbacks of application versions.

Here are some of the key features and benefits of using Deployments in Kubernetes:

Rolling Updates: Deployments can be used to manage rolling updates of application versions, ensuring that new versions are deployed gradually to minimize downtime and risk.

Rollbacks: Deployments can be used to manage rollbacks of application versions, allowing users to quickly and easily revert to a previous version in the event of an issue.

Scaling: Deployments can be used to manage the scaling of applications, ensuring that the desired number of replica Pods are running at all times.

Self-healing: Deployments can be used to manage the self-healing of applications, automatically replacing failed Pods with new replicas to maintain the desired state.

Here's an example of using kubectl to create a Deployment in Kubernetes:

```
apiVersion: apps/v1
kind: Deployment
metadata:
  name: my-app
spec:
  replicas: 3
  selector:
    matchLabels:
      app: my-app
  template:
    metadata:
      labels:
        app: my-app
    spec:
      containers:
      - name: my-container
        image: my-image:latest
        ports:
        - containerPort: 80
```

This Deployment creates three replicas of a Pod template that runs a container called my-container using the image my-image:latest. The selector field specifies that the Pods should be labeled with app: my-app, and the replicas field specifies that there should be three replicas running at all times.

Here's an example of using kubectl to update a Deployment in Kubernetes:

```
kubectl set image deployment/my-app my-container=my-image:2.0
```

This command updates the Deployment my-app to use version 2.0 of the my-image container.

In conclusion, a Deployment in Kubernetes is a higher-level abstraction that is used to manage the lifecycle of Pods. Deployments provide features such as rolling updates, rollbacks, scaling, and self-healing, making it easier to manage and maintain containerized applications in a Kubernetes cluster. Understanding how to use Deployments is essential for managing and deploying containerized applications in a Kubernetes cluster.

2.17   How do you expose an application in a Kubernetes cluster using a Service?

To expose an application in a Kubernetes cluster, you can use a Service. A Service is a Kubernetes resource that provides a stable IP address and DNS name for accessing a set of Pods in a deployment or replica set. By creating a Service, you can expose your application to the outside world or other services running in the cluster.

Here are the steps to expose an application in a Kubernetes cluster using a Service:

Create a Deployment: First, create a Deployment that specifies the Pod template for your application.

```
apiVersion: apps/v1
kind: Deployment
metadata:
  name: my-app
spec:
  replicas: 3
  selector:
    matchLabels:
      app: my-app
  template:
    metadata:
      labels:
        app: my-app
    spec:
      containers:
      - name: my-container
        image: my-image:latest
        ports:
        - containerPort: 80
```

Create a Service: Next, create a Service that targets the Pods in your Deployment. This will create a stable IP address and DNS name for accessing your application.

```
apiVersion: v1
kind: Service
metadata:
  name: my-service
spec:
  selector:
    app: my-app
  ports:
  - name: http
    port: 80
```

```
    targetPort: 80
  type: ClusterIP
```

This Service targets the Pods in the Deployment with the label app: my-app, and exposes port 80 for accessing the application. The type field is set to ClusterIP, which creates a virtual IP address for the Service that is only accessible within the cluster.

Access your application: Now that you have a Service created, you can access your application using the IP address or DNS name of the Service.

```
http://<service-ip>:<port>
```

In this example, you would replace <service-ip> with the IP address of the Service, and <port> with the port number you specified in the Service configuration (in this case, 80).

Alternatively, you can use the DNS name of the Service to access your application.

```
http://<service-name>.<namespace>.svc.cluster.local:<port>
```

In this example, you would replace <service-name> with the name of the Service, <namespace> with the namespace in which the Service was created, and <port> with the port number you specified in the Service configuration (in this case, 80).

In conclusion, to expose an application in a Kubernetes cluster using a Service, you need to create a Deployment that specifies the Pod template for your application, create a Service that targets the Pods in your Deployment, and then access your application using the IP address or DNS name of the Service. Services are an essential component of Kubernetes networking and provide a way to expose your applications to the outside world or other services running in the cluster.

2.18 Describe the key components of a Kubernetes manifest file.

A Kubernetes manifest file is a YAML or JSON file that is used to describe the desired state of Kubernetes resources in a cluster. A manifest file contains a set of instructions that Kubernetes can use to create, modify, or delete resources in the cluster.

Here are the key components of a Kubernetes manifest file:

API Version: The apiVersion field specifies the Kubernetes API version that is used by the manifest file. This field is required for all resources in the manifest file.

```
apiVersion: apps/v1
```

Kind: The kind field specifies the type of Kubernetes resource that is being defined in the manifest file. This field is required for all resources in the manifest file.

```
kind: Deployment
```

Metadata: The metadata field contains information about the resource, such as its name, labels, and annotations.

```
metadata:
  name: my-app
  labels:
    app: my-app
  annotations:
    build: 1
```

Spec: The spec field contains the specification for the Kubernetes resource, including the desired state of the resource and any configuration settings.

```
spec:
  replicas: 3
  selector:
    matchLabels:
      app: my-app
  template:
    metadata:
      labels:
        app: my-app
    spec:
      containers:
      - name: my-container
        image: my-image:latest
        ports:
        - containerPort: 80
```

The spec field for a Deployment, for example, contains information about the desired number of replicas, the selector used to identify the Pods in the Deployment, and the Pod template that specifies the container image and configuration.

In addition to these key components, a Kubernetes manifest file may also include other fields and settings that are specific to the type of resource being defined. For example, a Service resource may include a type field that specifies the type of Service to create, while a ConfigMap resource may include a data field that specifies the key-value pairs to include in the configuration.

Here's an example of a simple Kubernetes manifest file that defines a Deployment resource:

```
apiVersion: apps/v1
kind: Deployment
metadata:
  name: my-app
spec:
  replicas: 3
  selector:
    matchLabels:
      app: my-app
  template:
    metadata:
      labels:
        app: my-app
    spec:
      containers:
      - name: my-container
        image: my-image:latest
        ports:
        - containerPort: 80
```

This manifest file defines a Deployment resource called my-app that has three replicas and uses the container image my-image:latest with a port of 80.

In conclusion, a Kubernetes manifest file is a YAML or JSON file that is used to describe the desired state of Kubernetes resources in a cluster. The key components of a manifest file include the API version, the kind of resource being defined, the metadata for the resource, and the specification for the resource. By understanding the key components of a Kubernetes manifest file, you can create, modify, or delete resources in a Kubernetes cluster with ease.

2.19 What is Horizontal Pod Autoscaling (HPA) in Kubernetes and how does it work?

Horizontal Pod Autoscaling (HPA) is a Kubernetes feature that allows you to automatically scale the number of Pods in a Deployment or ReplicaSet based on resource utilization. With HPA, you can ensure that your application has enough resources to handle increasing traffic and load, while also reducing costs by scaling down when resources are not needed.

Here's how HPA works in Kubernetes:

Metrics Server: To use HPA, you first need to have a metrics server installed in your Kubernetes cluster. The metrics server collects resource utilization data for Pods, such as CPU and memory usage, and makes it available to other Kubernetes components.

HPA Configuration: Next, you need to create an HPA configuration that specifies the minimum and maximum number of Pods to run, as well as the target resource utilization. This is done using a YAML or JSON file that defines the HPA object.

```
apiVersion: autoscaling/v2beta2
kind: HorizontalPodAutoscaler
metadata:
  name: my-hpa
spec:
  scaleTargetRef:
    apiVersion: apps/v1
    kind: Deployment
    name: my-deployment
  minReplicas: 2
  maxReplicas: 10
  metrics:
  - type: Resource
    resource:
      name: cpu
      targetAverageUtilization: 50
```

This HPA configuration specifies that the Deployment called my-deployment should have between 2 and 10 replicas, and that the target resource utilization for CPU should be 50%. This means that if the CPU utilization of the Pods in the Deployment exceeds 50%, HPA will automatically scale up the number of replicas, and if the CPU utilization drops below 50%, HPA will scale down the number of replicas.

HPA Controller: Once you have created an HPA configuration, the HPA controller will continuously monitor the resource utilization of the Pods and adjust the number of replicas based on the target utilization. The HPA controller will also automatically adjust the number of replicas when changes are made to the HPA configuration or the Deployment configuration.

Here's an example of using kubectl to create an HPA configuration for a Deployment in Kubernetes:

```
kubectl autoscale deployment my-deployment --cpu-percent=50 --min=2
    --max=10
```

This command creates an HPA configuration for the Deployment my-deployment with a target CPU utilization of 50%, a minimum of 2 replicas, and a maximum of 10 replicas.

In conclusion, Horizontal Pod Autoscaling (HPA) in Kubernetes is a feature that allows you to automatically scale the number of Pods in a Deployment or ReplicaSet based on resource utilization. With HPA, you can ensure that your application has enough resources to handle increasing traffic and load, while also reducing costs by scaling down when resources are not needed. To use HPA, you need to have a metrics server installed, create an HPA configuration that specifies the minimum and maximum number of Pods and target resource utilization, and have the HPA controller continuously monitor the resource utilization and adjust the number of replicas accordingly.

2.20 Explain the difference between a LoadBalancer and a NodePort service type in Kubernetes.

In Kubernetes, a Service is an abstraction that provides a stable IP address and DNS name for accessing a set of Pods. There are several types of Services in Kubernetes, including ClusterIP, NodePort, and LoadBalancer.

NodePort and LoadBalancer are both types of Services that allow external traffic to access Pods in a Kubernetes cluster, but they have different use cases and functionality.

Here are the differences between a LoadBalancer and a NodePort Service type in Kubernetes:

LoadBalancer:

A LoadBalancer Service type is used to expose a Service externally, outside the cluster, to the internet or another network. Load-Balancer Services create an external load balancer in the cloud provider's network that forwards traffic to the Service. LoadBalancer Services are typically used when you need to expose a Service to the public internet, or when you need to distribute traffic evenly across multiple nodes in a cluster. LoadBalancer Services are often used in cloud environments, such as AWS, Google Cloud, or Azure, which provide load balancers as a managed service.

Here's an example of creating a LoadBalancer Service in Kubernetes:

```
apiVersion: v1
kind: Service
metadata:
  name: my-loadbalancer-service
spec:
  type: LoadBalancer
  selector:
    app: my-app
  ports:
  - name: http
    port: 80
    targetPort: 8080
```

This LoadBalancer Service exposes a Service called my-app with port 80 and forwards traffic to port 8080 on the Pods that match the selector app: my-app. When this Service is created, a load balancer is provisioned by the cloud provider to distribute traffic to the Pods.

NodePort:

A NodePort Service type is used to expose a Service on a specific port on all Nodes in a cluster.

NodePort Services create a high-numbered port on each Node in the cluster that forwards traffic to the Service.

NodePort Services are typically used when you need to expose a Service externally for testing or debugging purposes, or when you need to access the Service from outside the cluster, such as from a web browser or a command-line tool.

NodePort Services are not recommended for production use, as they can expose Pods directly to the internet without authentication or encryption.

Here's an example of creating a NodePort Service in Kubernetes:

```
apiVersion: v1
kind: Service
metadata:
  name: my-nodeport-service
spec:
  type: NodePort
  selector:
    app: my-app
  ports:
  - name: http
    port: 80
    targetPort: 8080
    nodePort: 30080
```

This NodePort Service exposes a Service called my-app with port 80 and forwards traffic to port 8080 on the Pods that match the selector app: my-app. The Service is also exposed on port 30080 on all Nodes in the cluster. When traffic is sent to port 30080 on a Node, it is forwarded to the Service on port 80.

In conclusion, LoadBalancer and NodePort are both types of Services in Kubernetes that allow external traffic to access Pods, but they have different use cases and functionality. LoadBalancer Services are used to expose a Service externally to the internet or another network, while NodePort Services are used to expose a Service on a specific port on all Nodes in a cluster.

Chapter 3

Intermediate

3.1 What is a Deployment in Kubernetes and how does it differ from a ReplicaSet?

In Kubernetes, a Deployment is a high-level API object that provides declarative updates for Pods and ReplicaSets. Deployments are used to manage the rollout and scaling of Pods in a declarative manner, making it easy to update and roll back changes.

A ReplicaSet, on the other hand, is a lower-level API object that ensures a specific number of replicas of a Pod are running at any given time. ReplicaSets are used to maintain the desired state of a Pod or set of Pods, and to replace Pods that have failed or been terminated.

Here are the main differences between a Deployment and a ReplicaSet in Kubernetes:

Deployment:

A Deployment is a higher-level API object that manages ReplicaSets and provides declarative updates to the desired state of Pods.

Deployments can be used to roll out changes to an application, such as updating the container image or changing the configuration, while ensuring that the application remains available during the update process.

Deployments support rolling updates, which update the Pods in a controlled and gradual manner to minimize downtime and disruptions.

Deployments can also be used to roll back changes to a previous version of the application if there are issues with the new version.

Deployments are usually used for stateless applications that can be scaled horizontally by adding or removing Pods.

Here's an example of creating a Deployment in Kubernetes:

```
apiVersion: apps/v1
kind: Deployment
metadata:
  name: my-deployment
spec:
  replicas: 3
  selector:
    matchLabels:
      app: my-app
  template:
    metadata:
      labels:
        app: my-app
    spec:
      containers:
      - name: my-container
        image: my-image:latest
        ports:
        - containerPort: 8080
```

This Deployment creates three replicas of a Pod template that runs a container called my-container with the image my-image:latest. The Pod template has a label of app: my-app, which is used to match the Pods created by the Deployment. The replicas field specifies that there should be three replicas of the Pod template running at all times.

ReplicaSet:

A ReplicaSet is a lower-level API object that ensures a specific number of replicas of a Pod are running at any given time.

ReplicaSets can be used to maintain the desired state of a Pod or set of Pods, and to replace Pods that have failed or been terminated.

ReplicaSets support scaling the number of replicas up or down, but they do not support rolling updates or rollbacks.

ReplicaSets are usually used for stateful applications that require a fixed number of replicas, such as a database or message queue.

Here's an example of creating a ReplicaSet in Kubernetes:

```
apiVersion: apps/v1
kind: ReplicaSet
metadata:
  name: my-replicaset
spec:
  replicas: 3
  selector:
    matchLabels:
      app: my-app
  template:
    metadata:
      labels:
        app: my-app
    spec:
      containers:
      - name: my-container
        image: my-image:latest
        ports:
        - containerPort: 8080
```

This ReplicaSet creates three replicas of a Pod template that runs a container called my-container with the image my-image:latest. The Pod template has a label of app: my-app, which is used to match the Pods created by the ReplicaSet. The replicas field specifies that there should be three replicas of the Pod template running at all times.

In conclusion, while both Deployments and ReplicaSets are used to manage the state of Pods in Kubernetes, Deployments provide a higher-level abstraction for managing the rollout and scaling

3.2 Explain the difference between a ConfigMap and a Secret, and when you should use each.

In Kubernetes, both ConfigMaps and Secrets are used to manage configuration data, but they differ in their use cases and how they handle sensitive data.

ConfigMap:

A ConfigMap is an API object used to store configuration data in key-value pairs that can be accessed by Pods in a Kubernetes cluster. ConfigMaps are used to separate configuration data from the application code and provide a way to update configuration data without rebuilding and redeploying the application.

Here are some use cases for ConfigMaps:

Storing environment variables and other configuration data for an application.

Providing configuration data to multiple containers running in a Pod.

Storing configuration data that needs to be changed frequently.

Here's an example of creating a ConfigMap in Kubernetes:

```
apiVersion: v1
kind: ConfigMap
metadata:
  name: my-configmap
data:
  DB_HOST: mydatabase.example.com
  DB_PORT: "5432"
```

This ConfigMap stores two key-value pairs, DB_HOST and DB_PORT, that can be accessed by Pods in the cluster.

Secret:

A Secret is an API object used to store sensitive data, such as passwords, API keys, and other secrets, in a secure manner. Secrets are similar to ConfigMaps, but they are base64-encoded and stored encrypted in etcd, the Kubernetes data store. Secrets are mounted as files or environment variables in a Pod, just like ConfigMaps.

Here are some use cases for Secrets:

Storing sensitive data, such as passwords and API keys, for an application.

Providing sensitive data to multiple containers running in a Pod.

Storing data that needs to be accessed by Pods securely.

Here's an example of creating a Secret in Kubernetes:

```
apiVersion: v1
kind: Secret
metadata:
  name: my-secret
type: Opaque
data:
  password: cGFzc3dvcmQxMjM=
```

This Secret stores a single key-value pair, password, which is base64-encoded. The type: Opaque field specifies that the Secret should be stored in an opaque format, meaning that the data is encrypted and not interpreted by Kubernetes.

When to use ConfigMaps vs. Secrets:

ConfigMaps should be used for non-sensitive configuration data that needs to be accessed by Pods, while Secrets should be used for sensitive data that needs to be accessed by Pods securely. Both ConfigMaps and Secrets can be used to provide configuration data to multiple containers running in a Pod.

In conclusion, ConfigMaps and Secrets are both used to manage configuration data in Kubernetes, but they differ in their use cases and how they handle sensitive data. ConfigMaps are used for non-sensitive configuration data, while Secrets are used for sensitive data that needs to be accessed securely.

3.3 Describe the process of rolling updates in Kubernetes and its advantages.

In Kubernetes, rolling updates are a way to update a deployment, stateful set, or daemon set in a controlled and gradual manner. Rolling updates update the Pods in a controlled and gradual manner to minimize downtime and disruptions.

The process of rolling updates in Kubernetes involves the following steps:

Update the container image or configuration: The first step in a rolling update is to update the container image or configuration that you want to deploy. This can be done by editing the YAML manifest file for the deployment or stateful set.

Create a new replica set: Once the updated configuration is in place, a new replica set is created with the updated configuration. The new replica set runs alongside the old one, allowing for a controlled transition between the old and new versions of the application.

Scale up the new replica set: The next step is to gradually scale up the new replica set while scaling down the old one. This ensures that the application remains available during the update process.

Monitor the update process: Throughout the rolling update process, Kubernetes monitors the status of the Pods in both the old and new replica sets. If any of the new Pods fail to start or the old Pods fail to terminate, Kubernetes will pause the rolling update and roll back to the previous version of the application.

Complete the update: Once all of the new Pods are running and the old Pods have been terminated, the rolling update is complete and the new version of the application is running.

Advantages of rolling updates in Kubernetes:

Minimize downtime: Rolling updates allow for a controlled and gradual transition between the old and new versions of the application, minimizing downtime and disruptions.

Maintain availability: By running the old and new versions of the application side-by-side, rolling updates ensure that the application remains available during the update process.

Rollback if necessary: Kubernetes monitors the update process and can automatically roll back to the previous version of the application if any issues arise.

Scalability: Rolling updates can be used to scale up or down the number of replicas of the application, allowing for easy horizontal scaling.

Here's an example of a rolling update in Kubernetes:

```
apiVersion: apps/v1
kind: Deployment
metadata:
  name: my-deployment
spec:
  replicas: 3
  selector:
    matchLabels:
      app: my-app
  template:
    metadata:
      labels:
        app: my-app
    spec:
      containers:
      - name: my-container
        image: my-image:v1
        ports:
        - containerPort: 8080
  strategy:
    type: RollingUpdate
    rollingUpdate:
      maxSurge: 1
      maxUnavailable: 1
\# Update the image to v2
\# to perform a rolling update
\# on the deployment.
\# Use "kubectl apply" to apply
\# the changes to the deployment.
\# kubectl apply -f deployment.yaml
```

In this example, the YAML manifest file for the deployment is updated to use a new container image, my-image:v2. When the updated manifest file is applied using kubectl apply -f deployment.yaml, Kubernetes will perform a rolling update by creating a new replica set with the updated configuration and gradually scaling it up while scaling down the old replica set.

3.4 How does Kubernetes handle container resource management, such as CPU and memory limits?

In Kubernetes, container resource management is handled through resource requests and limits.

Resource requests specify the minimum amount of resources that a container requires to run, while resource limits specify the maximum amount of resources that a container can use. By setting resource requests and limits, Kubernetes can ensure that containers have access to the resources they need and prevent them from using too many resources and disrupting other containers running on the same node.

CPU limits:

Kubernetes allows you to set CPU limits for containers using the resources field in the YAML manifest file for the Pod or Deployment. For example, to set a CPU limit of 0.5 CPU cores for a container, you can add the following to the manifest file:

```
apiVersion: v1
kind: Pod
metadata:
  name: my-pod
spec:
  containers:
  - name: my-container
    image: my-image
    resources:
      limits:
        cpu: 500m
```

In this example, the resources.limits.cpu field is set to 500m, which means that the container is limited to using 0.5 CPU cores.

Memory limits:

Kubernetes allows you to set memory limits for containers using the resources field in the YAML manifest file for the Pod or Deployment. For example, to set a memory limit of 512 MB for a container, you can add the following to the manifest file:

```
apiVersion: v1
kind: Pod
metadata:
```

```
    name: my-pod
spec:
  containers:
  - name: my-container
    image: my-image
    resources:
      limits:
        memory: 512Mi
```

In this example, the resources.limits.memory field is set to 512Mi, which means that the container is limited to using 512 MB of memory.

Resource requests:

Kubernetes also allows you to set resource requests for containers using the resources field in the YAML manifest file. Resource requests specify the minimum amount of resources that a container requires to run, and Kubernetes uses this information to schedule containers on nodes that have enough resources to meet the requests. For example, to set a CPU request of 0.25 CPU cores and a memory request of 256 MB for a container, you can add the following to the manifest file:

```
apiVersion: v1
kind: Pod
metadata:
  name: my-pod
spec:
  containers:
  - name: my-container
    image: my-image
    resources:
      requests:
        cpu: 250m
        memory: 256Mi
```

In this example, the resources.requests.cpu field is set to 250m, which means that the container requires at least 0.25 CPU cores to run, and the resources.requests.memory field is set to 256Mi, which means that the container requires at least 256 MB of memory to run.

In conclusion, Kubernetes uses resource requests and limits to manage container resource usage, preventing containers from using too many resources and disrupting other containers running on the same node. By setting resource requests and limits, you can ensure that your containers have access to the resources they need and prevent them from using too many resources and causing performance issues.

3.5 Explain the role of a Kubernetes Ingress and how it differs from a Service.

In Kubernetes, a Service is used to provide network access to a set of pods, allowing them to communicate with each other and with the outside world. A Service can be exposed using various types, such as ClusterIP, NodePort, and LoadBalancer.

However, when you want to expose multiple services to the outside world using a single IP address, you can use a Kubernetes Ingress. An Ingress is a Kubernetes resource that acts as a layer 7 load balancer, providing routing and TLS termination for HTTP and HTTPS traffic.

An Ingress resource defines rules for how incoming traffic should be directed to backend Services based on the incoming host, path, and other information in the request. The rules can be configured to send traffic to different Services based on the incoming URL, host, or other factors.

For example, the following Ingress resource directs incoming traffic to different Services based on the incoming URL:

```
apiVersion: networking.k8s.io/v1
kind: Ingress
metadata:
  name: my-ingress
spec:
  rules:
  - host: example.com
    http:
      paths:
      - path: /app1
        pathType: Prefix
        backend:
          service:
            name: app1-service
            port:
              number: 80
      - path: /app2
        pathType: Prefix
        backend:
          service:
            name: app2-service
```

```
port:
    number: 80
```

In this example, incoming traffic to example.com/app1 will be directed to the app1-service Service, and incoming traffic to example.com/app2 will be directed to the app2-service Service.

In contrast to a Service, which only provides network access to a set of pods, an Ingress provides a higher level of network functionality, allowing you to route traffic based on incoming host and URL information. This makes it easier to expose multiple services using a single IP address and to manage traffic routing and load balancing for multiple services.

In conclusion, a Kubernetes Ingress is a layer 7 load balancer that provides routing and TLS termination for HTTP and HTTPS traffic, allowing you to expose multiple services using a single IP address and to manage traffic routing and load balancing for multiple services based on incoming host and URL information.

3.6 Describe the concept of Kubernetes init containers and their use cases.

In Kubernetes, an init container is a special type of container that is run before the main application container in a Pod. The main purpose of an init container is to perform some setup or initialization tasks that the application container requires before it can start running.

Init containers have their own container image and configuration, and are defined in the same YAML manifest file as the main application container. They can run commands or scripts to perform various initialization tasks, such as downloading data from an external source, populating a configuration file, or waiting for a database to become available.

One use case for init containers is to populate a shared volume with data that multiple containers in a Pod require. For example, you might have an application that requires a configuration file, and you want to generate this configuration file dynamically at startup time. An init container can be used to generate the configuration file and write it to a shared volume, which can then be mounted by the main application container.

Another use case for init containers is to perform a pre-flight check or validation before the main application container starts running. For example, you might have an application that requires a specific environment variable to be set, and you want to check that the environment variable is set correctly before the application starts. An init container can be used to perform the validation and exit with an error if the validation fails, preventing the main application container from starting.

Here is an example of a YAML manifest file that defines an init container that populates a shared volume with data that the main application container requires:

```
apiVersion: v1
kind: Pod
metadata:
  name: my-pod
spec:
  containers:
  - name: my-container
    image: my-image
    volumeMounts:
    - name: data-volume
      mountPath: /data
  initContainers:
  - name: init-container
    image: busybox
    command: ['sh', '-c', 'echo "Hello, world!" > /data/myfile']
    volumeMounts:
    - name: data-volume
      mountPath: /data
  volumes:
  - name: data-volume
    emptyDir: {}
```

In this example, the init container writes the message "Hello, world!" to a file called myfile in the /data directory, which is mounted as a shared volume by the main application container.

In conclusion, init containers are a useful feature of Kubernetes that allow you to perform initialization tasks and setup before the main application container starts running. They can be used to populate shared volumes, perform pre-flight checks, or perform any other tasks that are required before the main application container can start running.

3.7   What is a readiness probe and a liveness probe in Kubernetes, and why are they important?

In Kubernetes, readiness probes and liveness probes are mechanisms that allow you to check the health of your containerized applications running in Pods. These probes are important because they help ensure that your application is running correctly and can help prevent unexpected downtime or crashes.

A readiness probe is used to determine when a container is ready to start receiving traffic. When a Pod is created or updated, Kubernetes will wait until the readiness probe returns a success status before it starts routing traffic to the Pod. This ensures that your application is fully ready to handle incoming requests before it starts receiving traffic.

A liveness probe is used to determine when a container is still running correctly. Kubernetes will periodically check the status of the liveness probe, and if it returns a failure status, Kubernetes will automatically restart the container. This ensures that your application is always running and can help prevent downtime or crashes due to unexpected failures.

Both readiness probes and liveness probes are defined in the Pod specification using YAML files. Here is an example of a Pod specification with both readiness and liveness probes:

```
apiVersion: v1
kind: Pod
metadata:
  name: my-pod
spec:
  containers:
  - name: my-container
    image: my-image
    readinessProbe:
      httpGet:
        path: /healthz
        port: 8080
      initialDelaySeconds: 5
      periodSeconds: 10
    livenessProbe:
      httpGet:
        path: /healthz
        port: 8080
      initialDelaySeconds: 15
      periodSeconds: 20
```

In this example, the readiness probe and liveness probe are both defined using an HTTP GET request to the /healthz endpoint on port 8080. The readiness probe has an initial delay of 5 seconds and is checked every 10 seconds, while the liveness probe has an initial delay of 15 seconds and is checked every 20 seconds.

In conclusion, readiness probes and liveness probes are important mechanisms in Kubernetes that allow you to check the health of your containerized applications running in Pods. These probes help ensure that your application is running correctly and can help prevent unexpected downtime or crashes. By defining readiness and liveness probes in your Pod specification, you can take advantage of these powerful features and help ensure that your applications are always running smoothly.

3.8 How does Kubernetes handle storage using Persistent Volumes (PV) and Persistent Volume Claims (PVC)?

In Kubernetes, Persistent Volumes (PVs) and Persistent Volume Claims (PVCs) are used to provide persistent storage for containerized applications. PVs are networked storage resources that are provisioned by an administrator and made available to the cluster, while PVCs are requests for storage resources made by users or applications.

The process of using PVs and PVCs involves the following steps:

Provision a Persistent Volume: An administrator creates a PV by defining its properties, such as capacity, access mode, and storage class. The PV can be backed by various types of storage resources, such as local storage, network file systems, or cloud storage.

Create a Persistent Volume Claim: A user or application creates a PVC by specifying the desired amount of storage, access mode, and storage class. The PVC is a request for a specific amount of storage that matches the properties of a PV.

Bind the Persistent Volume Claim to a Persistent Volume: When a

PVC is created, Kubernetes searches for a suitable PV that matches the storage request. If a suitable PV is found, Kubernetes binds the PVC to the PV.

Mount the Persistent Volume to a Container: Once a PVC is bound to a PV, it can be mounted to a container in a Pod as a volume. The container can then read from and write to the volume as if it were a local file system.

Here is an example of how to create a PV and a PVC using YAML files:

```
\# persistent-volume.yaml
apiVersion: v1
kind: PersistentVolume
metadata:
  name: my-pv
spec:
  capacity:
    storage: 1Gi
  accessModes:
  - ReadWriteOnce
  persistentVolumeReclaimPolicy: Retain
  storageClassName: my-storage-class
  hostPath:
    path: /data

\# persistent-volume-claim.yaml
apiVersion: v1
kind: PersistentVolumeClaim
metadata:
  name: my-pvc
spec:
  accessModes:
  - ReadWriteOnce
  resources:
    requests:
      storage: 1Gi
  storageClassName: my-storage-class
```

In this example, we create a PV with a capacity of 1 gigabyte and a host path of /data. We also create a PVC that requests 1 gigabyte of storage and uses the my-storage-class storage class. The PVC is bound to the PV based on its capacity and storage class.

In conclusion, Kubernetes provides a powerful and flexible storage system using Persistent Volumes (PVs) and Persistent Volume Claims (PVCs). By using PVs and PVCs, users and applications can request and use storage resources in a standard and consistent way, regardless of the underlying storage technology. This allows Kubernetes to provide a unified storage management experience, whether the storage resources are local, networked, or cloud-based.

3.9   Explain the concept of affinity and anti-affinity rules in Kubernetes.

In Kubernetes, affinity and anti-affinity rules are used to specify the relationship between Pods and the nodes they are scheduled on. Affinity rules specify that Pods should be scheduled on nodes that match certain criteria, while anti-affinity rules specify that Pods should not be scheduled on nodes that match certain criteria.

Affinity rules and anti-affinity rules are defined using labels and selectors in the Pod specification. Here is an example of a Pod specification with an affinity rule:

```
apiVersion: v1
kind: Pod
metadata:
  name: my-pod
spec:
  containers:
  - name: my-container
    image: my-image
  nodeSelector:
    disktype: ssd
```

In this example, the nodeSelector field is used to specify an affinity rule that requires the Pod to be scheduled on a node with the label disktype=ssd. This ensures that the Pod is scheduled on a node with a solid-state drive (SSD) instead of a traditional hard disk drive (HDD).

Here is an example of a Pod specification with an anti-affinity rule:

```
apiVersion: v1
kind: Pod
metadata:
  name: my-pod
spec:
  containers:
  - name: my-container
    image: my-image
  affinity:
    podAntiAffinity:
      requiredDuringSchedulingIgnoredDuringExecution:
      - labelSelector:
          matchExpressions:
          - key: app
            operator: In
            values:
            - my-app
        topologyKey: kubernetes.io/hostname
```

In this example, the affinity field is used to specify an anti-affinity rule that requires the Pod to not be scheduled on a node that already has a Pod with the label app=my-app. The topologyKey field is used to specify that the rule should be enforced at the hostname level.

Affinity and anti-affinity rules can be used to achieve a variety of scheduling goals, such as ensuring that Pods are scheduled on nodes with certain resources, distributing Pods across multiple availability zones or regions, or preventing Pods from being scheduled on nodes that already have other Pods running. By using these rules, Kubernetes can provide a flexible and powerful scheduling system that can be tailored to the specific needs of each application or workload.

3.10   How do you monitor the health of a Kubernetes cluster and its components?

Monitoring the health of a Kubernetes cluster and its components is critical for ensuring the availability and reliability of applications running in the cluster. Kubernetes provides several built-in mechanisms for monitoring the health of the cluster and its components.

One of the primary mechanisms for monitoring the health of a Kubernetes cluster is through the use of Kubernetes Health Checks. Kubernetes provides two types of Health Checks: Liveness Probes and Readiness Probes.

Liveness Probes are used to determine whether a container in a Pod is still running. If a container fails a liveness probe, Kubernetes will restart the container. Readiness Probes are used to determine whether a container in a Pod is ready to serve traffic. If a container fails a readiness probe, Kubernetes will remove the Pod from the list of endpoints for the corresponding Service.

Here is an example of a Pod specification with both liveness and readiness probes:

```
apiVersion: v1
kind: Pod
metadata:
  name: my-pod
spec:
  containers:
  - name: my-container
    image: my-image
    livenessProbe:
      httpGet:
        path: /healthz
        port: 8080
      initialDelaySeconds: 5
      periodSeconds: 10
    readinessProbe:
      httpGet:
        path: /readyz
        port: 8080
      initialDelaySeconds: 5
      periodSeconds: 10
```

In this example, the livenessProbe and readinessProbe fields are used to specify HTTP endpoints /healthz and /readyz respectively, and their corresponding ports. The initialDelaySeconds field is used to specify a delay before the first probe is performed, and the periodSeconds field is used to specify the interval between successive probes.

Kubernetes also provides a built-in dashboard called Kubernetes Dashboard for monitoring the health of a cluster and its components. The Kubernetes Dashboard provides an overview of the cluster, including information on Nodes, Pods, Services, and Deployments. It also provides access to detailed metrics and logs for individual components.

Finally, there are several third-party monitoring tools that can be used to monitor the health of a Kubernetes cluster, such as Prometheus, Grafana, and Datadog. These tools provide advanced features for monitoring and alerting, including support for custom metrics, dashboards, and alerts.

In conclusion, monitoring the health of a Kubernetes cluster and its components is critical for ensuring the availability and reliability of applications running in the cluster. Kubernetes provides several built-in mechanisms for monitoring the health of the cluster and its components, including Health Checks, Kubernetes Dashboard, and third-party monitoring tools. By using these tools, operators can gain visibility into the health and performance of their Kubernetes clusters and take proactive steps to prevent issues before they impact their applications.

3.11 Describe the process of updating a running Kubernetes application with zero downtime.

Monitoring the health of a Kubernetes cluster and its components is critical for ensuring the availability and reliability of applications running in the cluster. Kubernetes provides several built-in mechanisms for monitoring the health of the cluster and its components.

One of the primary mechanisms for monitoring the health of a Kubernetes cluster is through the use of Kubernetes Health Checks. Kubernetes provides two types of Health Checks: Liveness Probes and Readiness Probes.

Liveness Probes are used to determine whether a container in a Pod is still running. If a container fails a liveness probe, Kubernetes will restart the container. Readiness Probes are used to determine whether a container in a Pod is ready to serve traffic. If a container fails a readiness probe, Kubernetes will remove the Pod from the list of endpoints for the corresponding Service.

Here is an example of a Pod specification with both liveness and readiness probes:

```
apiVersion: v1
kind: Pod
metadata:
  name: my-pod
spec:
  containers:
  - name: my-container
    image: my-image
    livenessProbe:
      httpGet:
        path: /healthz
        port: 8080
      initialDelaySeconds: 5
      periodSeconds: 10
    readinessProbe:
      httpGet:
        path: /readyz
```

```
    port: 8080
initialDelaySeconds: 5
periodSeconds: 10
```

In this example, the livenessProbe and readinessProbe fields are used to specify HTTP endpoints /healthz and /readyz respectively, and their corresponding ports. The initialDelaySeconds field is used to specify a delay before the first probe is performed, and the periodSeconds field is used to specify the interval between successive probes.

Kubernetes also provides a built-in dashboard called Kubernetes Dashboard for monitoring the health of a cluster and its components. The Kubernetes Dashboard provides an overview of the cluster, including information on Nodes, Pods, Services, and Deployments. It also provides access to detailed metrics and logs for individual components.

Finally, there are several third-party monitoring tools that can be used to monitor the health of a Kubernetes cluster, such as Prometheus, Grafana, and Datadog. These tools provide advanced features for monitoring and alerting, including support for custom metrics, dashboards, and alerts.

In conclusion, monitoring the health of a Kubernetes cluster and its components is critical for ensuring the availability and reliability of applications running in the cluster. Kubernetes provides several built-in mechanisms for monitoring the health of the cluster and its components, including Health Checks, Kubernetes Dashboard, and third-party monitoring tools. By using these tools, operators can gain visibility into the health and performance of their Kubernetes clusters and take proactive steps to prevent issues before they impact their applications.

3.12 What is a StatefulSet in Kubernetes and when should you use it?

In Kubernetes, a StatefulSet is a controller that manages the deployment and scaling of a set of stateful Pods. Unlike a Deployment, which manages stateless Pods that can be scaled up or down without any impact on application state, a StatefulSet is designed to manage stateful applications, such as databases or other stateful services, that require stable network identities and persistent storage.

Here are some of the key features and use cases of a StatefulSet in Kubernetes:

Stable Network Identity: Each Pod in a StatefulSet is given a unique and stable hostname that can be used to access the Pod within the cluster. This is critical for stateful applications that require stable network identities, such as databases or other services that rely on peer-to-peer communication.

Ordered Deployment: When a StatefulSet is created, the Pods are deployed in a specific order, based on their ordinal index. This ensures that the Pods are deployed and initialized in the correct order, which is important for stateful applications that have dependencies on other Pods in the set.

Persistent Storage: StatefulSets support the use of Persistent Volumes (PVs) and Persistent Volume Claims (PVCs) to provide persistent storage for stateful applications. This allows stateful applications to maintain their state across Pod restarts or scaling events.

Scaling: StatefulSets support scaling operations, such as scaling up or down the number of replicas. However, scaling down a StatefulSet is more complex than scaling down a Deployment, as it requires careful consideration of the application's state and dependencies.

Here is an example of a StatefulSet specification for a MySQL database:

```
apiVersion: apps/v1
kind: StatefulSet
metadata:
  name: mysql
spec:
  selector:
    matchLabels:
      app: mysql
  serviceName: mysql
  replicas: 3
  template:
    metadata:
      labels:
```

```
      app: mysql
spec:
  containers:
  - name: mysql
    image: mysql:5.7
    env:
    - name: MYSQL\_ROOT\_PASSWORD
      valueFrom:
        secretKeyRef:
          name: mysql-secrets
          key: mysql-root-password
    ports:
    - containerPort: 3306
    volumeMounts:
    - name: mysql-persistent-storage
      mountPath: /var/lib/mysql
volumeClaimTemplates:
- metadata:
    name: mysql-persistent-storage
  spec:
    accessModes: [ "ReadWriteOnce" ]
    resources:
      requests:
        storage: 1Gi
```

In this example, the StatefulSet specifies a MySQL database with three replicas, each with a unique and stable hostname. The StatefulSet also specifies the use of Persistent Volumes for persistent storage, and the use of a Secret for storing the MySQL root password.

In conclusion, a StatefulSet in Kubernetes is a controller that manages the deployment and scaling of a set of stateful Pods. StatefulSets are designed for stateful applications, such as databases or other stateful services, that require stable network identities and persistent storage. By providing features such as stable network identities, ordered deployment, and persistent storage, StatefulSets enable the deployment of stateful applications in a Kubernetes cluster with ease.

3.13 Explain the process of rolling back a Deployment in Kubernetes.

Rolling back a Deployment in Kubernetes is a straightforward process that can be done using the kubectl command-line tool. Here are the steps involved:

View the history of the Deployment: Use the following command to view the history of the Deployment:

```
kubectl rollout history deployment/<deployment-name>
```

This command will display a list of revisions for the Deployment, along with information such as the revision number, the date and time of the revision, and any annotations associated with the revision.

Roll back to a specific revision: Once you have identified the revision you want to roll back to, use the following command to initiate the rollback:

```
kubectl rollout undo deployment/<deployment-name> --to-revision=<
    revision-number>
```

This command will initiate a rollback to the specified revision. Kubernetes will automatically update the replicas of the Deployment to the previous version.

Monitor the progress of the rollback: Use the following command to monitor the progress of the rollback:

```
kubectl rollout status deployment/<deployment-name>
```

This command will display the status of the Deployment, including the number of replicas that are up and running, and the progress of the rollout.

Verify the rollback: Once the rollback is complete, use the following command to verify that the Deployment has been rolled back to the previous version:

```
kubectl get deployment/<deployment-name> -o yaml | grep -A 2 image:
```

This command will display the image tag used by each replica of the Deployment. Verify that the image tag matches the previous version.

Here is an example of rolling back a Deployment to a previous revision:

```
\# View the history of the Deployment
kubectl rollout history deployment/myapp
\# Roll back to a specific revision
kubectl rollout undo deployment/myapp --to-revision=2
```

```
\# Monitor the progress of the rollback
kubectl rollout status deployment/myapp

\# Verify the rollback
kubectl get deployment/myapp -o yaml | grep -A 2 image:
```

In conclusion, rolling back a Deployment in Kubernetes is a simple process that can be done using the kubectl command-line tool. By following the steps outlined above, you can quickly and easily roll back a Deployment to a previous version.

3.14 What are Kubernetes Jobs and Cron-Jobs, and what are their primary use cases?

Kubernetes provides two different controllers to manage batch workloads: Jobs and CronJobs. Let's explore their definitions and use cases below.

Kubernetes Jobs

A Job in Kubernetes is a controller object that runs a pod or set of pods to completion. It is used for performing batch processing, such as running a script or a container that performs a task and exits when it is completed. Once the task is finished, the pod or set of pods is terminated.

The Job controller ensures that the pod or set of pods are created and scheduled correctly. It monitors the status of the pods and retries them if they fail, ensuring that the task is completed successfully. Jobs are typically used for running one-time or intermittent tasks, such as running a backup or running a script to update data in a database.

Here's an example of a Job manifest file:

```
apiVersion: batch/v1
kind: Job
metadata:
  name: myjob
spec:
  template:
    spec:
```

```
containers:
- name: myjob
  image: myimage:latest
  command: ["python"]
  args: ["myjob.py"]
restartPolicy: OnFailure
backoffLimit: 4
```

In this example, we define a Job called myjob that runs a container based on the myimage:latest image, which executes a Python script called myjob.py. The restartPolicy is set to OnFailure, which means that if the pod fails to run, it will be restarted up to four times before the Job is marked as failed.

Kubernetes CronJobs

A CronJob in Kubernetes is a controller object that runs a Job on a scheduled basis. It is used for running periodic or recurring tasks, such as running a backup every night or running a data analysis job every week.

CronJobs are created using a cron expression, which specifies the schedule for running the Job. The Job controller ensures that the Job is created and scheduled at the correct time based on the cron expression.

Here's an example of a CronJob manifest file:

```
apiVersion: batch/v1beta1
kind: CronJob
metadata:
  name: mycronjob
spec:
  schedule: "*/5 * * * *"
  jobTemplate:
    spec:
      template:
        spec:
          containers:
          - name: myjob
            image: myimage:latest
            command: ["python"]
            args: ["myjob.py"]
          restartPolicy: OnFailure
successfulJobsHistoryLimit: 3
```

In this example, we define a CronJob called mycronjob that runs a Job every five minutes. The Job runs a container based on the myimage:latest image, which executes a Python script called myjob.py. The restartPolicy is set to OnFailure, and the successfulJobsHistoryLimit is set to 3, which means that up to three successful Job runs will be kept in the history.

In conclusion, Kubernetes Jobs and CronJobs are two powerful controllers that enable batch processing and periodic or recurring tasks in a Kubernetes cluster. Jobs are used for running one-time or intermittent tasks, while CronJobs are used for running periodic or recurring tasks based on a schedule. By leveraging these controllers, you can easily automate various tasks in your Kubernetes cluster.

3.15 Describe the process of autoscaling in Kubernetes using the Horizontal Pod Autoscaler (HPA) and the Cluster Autoscaler.

Kubernetes provides two different mechanisms for autoscaling: the Horizontal Pod Autoscaler (HPA) and the Cluster Autoscaler. Let's explore the process of autoscaling using each of these mechanisms below.

Horizontal Pod Autoscaler (HPA)

The Horizontal Pod Autoscaler (HPA) is a Kubernetes feature that enables you to automatically scale the number of pods in a Deployment or ReplicaSet based on CPU utilization or custom metrics. It works by continuously monitoring the resource utilization of the pods and adjusting the number of replicas accordingly.

Here's the process of configuring and using HPA:

Enable the metrics-server addon:

```
kubectl apply -f https://github.com/kubernetes-sigs/metrics-server/
    releases/latest/download/components.yaml
```

Define the HPA manifest file. For example, let's say we have a Deployment with the name my-deployment, which runs a container that exposes an HTTP server. We want to scale the number of replicas based on CPU utilization, with a target of 50% CPU usage per pod:

```
apiVersion: autoscaling/v2beta2
kind: HorizontalPodAutoscaler
metadata:
  name: my-hpa
spec:
  scaleTargetRef:
    apiVersion: apps/v1
    kind: Deployment
    name: my-deployment
  minReplicas: 1
  maxReplicas: 10
  metrics:
  - type: Resource
    resource:
      name: cpu
      target:
        type: Utilization
        averageUtilization: 50
```

In this example, we define an HPA called my-hpa that targets the my-deployment Deployment. We set the minimum number of replicas to 1 and the maximum number to 10. We also define a metric based on CPU utilization, with a target of 50% CPU usage per pod.

Apply the HPA manifest file:

```
kubectl apply -f my-hpa.yaml
```

This will create the HPA and start monitoring the CPU utilization of the pods in the my-deployment Deployment.

Verify the HPA:

```
kubectl get hpa
```

This will show the status of the HPA, including the current number of replicas, the target CPU utilization, and the actual CPU utilization.

Cluster Autoscaler

The Cluster Autoscaler is a Kubernetes feature that enables you to automatically scale the number of nodes in a cluster based on resource utilization. It works by continuously monitoring the resource utilization of the nodes and adding or removing nodes as needed.

Here's the process of configuring and using the Cluster Autoscaler:

Enable the Cluster Autoscaler addon:

```
kubectl apply -f https://github.com/kubernetes/autoscaler/
    releases/latest/download/cluster-autoscaler.yml
```

Configure the Cluster Autoscaler to use your cloud provider's API
for scaling. For example, if you're using AWS, you can create an
IAM policy and role for the Cluster Autoscaler to use:

```
\# Create the IAM policy
cat > cluster-autoscaler-policy.json <<EOF
{
    "Version": "2012-10-17",
    "Statement": [
        {
            "Effect": "Allow",
            "Action": [
                "autoscaling:DescribeAutoScalingGroups",
                "autoscaling:DescribeAutoScalingInstances",
                "autoscaling:DescribeLaunchConfigurations",
                "autoscaling:DescribeTags",
                "autoscaling:SetDesiredCapacity",
                "autoscaling:TerminateInstanceInAutoScalingGroup"
            ],
            "Resource": "*"
        }
    ]
}
EOF
```

3.16   How can you use Helm to manage application deployments in Kubernetes?

Helm is a package manager for Kubernetes that simplifies the process of installing, upgrading, and managing applications in a Kubernetes cluster. Helm packages are called charts, and they include
all the resources necessary to deploy an application, such as Kubernetes manifests, configuration files, and dependencies.

Here's how you can use Helm to manage application deployments
in Kubernetes:

Install Helm:

```
curl https://raw.githubusercontent.com/helm/helm/master/scripts/get-
    helm-3 | bash
```

Create a new Helm chart:

```
helm create mychart
```

This will create a new directory called mychart, which contains the files for the chart.

Edit the values.yaml file to set the configuration options for the application.

For example, let's say we're deploying a simple web application that listens on port 8080. We can set the port number in the values.yaml file like this:

```
service:
  port: 8080
```

Add any necessary Kubernetes resources to the chart, such as Deployments, Services, and ConfigMaps.

For example, let's say we have a Deployment that runs a container with the image myimage:latest, and we want to expose it using a Service. We can add the following to the templates/deployment.yaml file:

```
apiVersion: apps/v1
kind: Deployment
metadata:
  name: {{ .Chart.Name }}
  labels:
    app: {{ .Chart.Name }}
spec:
  replicas: 1
  selector:
    matchLabels:
      app: {{ .Chart.Name }}
  template:
    metadata:
      labels:
        app: {{ .Chart.Name }}
    spec:
      containers:
        - name: {{ .Chart.Name }}
          image: myimage:latest
          ports:
            - containerPort: 8080
```

And we can add the following to the templates/service.yaml file:

```
apiVersion: v1
kind: Service
metadata:
  name: {{ .Chart.Name }}
```

```
spec:
  selector:
    app: {{ .Chart.Name }}
  ports:
    - port: {{ .Values.service.port }}
      targetPort: 8080
  type: ClusterIP
```

This will create a Deployment with one replica that runs the my-image:latest container and a Service that exposes it on port 8080.

Package the chart:

```
helm package mychart
```

This will create a mychart.tgz file, which is the packaged chart.

Install the chart in a Kubernetes cluster:

```
helm install myrelease mychart.tgz
```

This will install the chart in a new release called myrelease.

Verify the deployment:

```
kubectl get deployments,services
```

This will show the status of the Deployment and Service created by the chart.

Upgrade the chart:

If you need to make changes to the chart, you can upgrade it using the following command:

```
helm upgrade myrelease mychart.tgz
```

This will upgrade the chart to the latest version and apply any changes you've made.

Helm simplifies the process of managing application deployments in Kubernetes by providing a standardized way to package, install, and upgrade applications. It also enables you to easily share and reuse charts with others in your organization.

3.17 Explain the difference between imperative, declarative, and hybrid approaches in managing Kubernetes resources.

In Kubernetes, there are different approaches to manage resources such as Pods, Services, Deployments, and ConfigMaps. These approaches are known as the imperative, declarative, and hybrid approaches.

Imperative Approach

The imperative approach to Kubernetes resource management is a command-based approach. It involves using commands to create, update, or delete resources in the cluster. This approach is ideal for simple and one-time operations. It is also suitable for quick testing of resources before creating manifests.

An example of creating a deployment imperatively is:

```
kubectl create deployment nginx --image=nginx:latest
```

This command creates a deployment named "nginx" using the latest version of the Nginx image from Docker Hub.

Declarative Approach

The declarative approach to Kubernetes resource management is a YAML-based approach. It involves creating a YAML file that specifies the desired state of the resource, and then applying it to the cluster. This approach is suitable for managing resources in production environments because it provides an audit trail of changes made to resources.

An example of creating a deployment declaratively is:

```
apiVersion: apps/v1
kind: Deployment
metadata:
  name: nginx
spec:
  replicas: 3
  selector:
    matchLabels:
      app: nginx
```

```
template:
  metadata:
    labels:
      app: nginx
  spec:
    containers:
    - name: nginx
      image: nginx:latest
```

This YAML file specifies a deployment named "nginx" with three replicas and uses the Nginx image from Docker Hub. It also specifies the selector and labels for the deployment.

To apply this YAML file to the cluster, you can use the command:

```
kubectl apply -f nginx-deployment.yaml
```

Hybrid Approach

The hybrid approach to Kubernetes resource management combines the imperative and declarative approaches. It involves creating a YAML file that specifies the desired state of the resource, and then using imperative commands to make changes to the resource as needed. This approach is suitable for managing resources in a more dynamic environment, where changes need to be made frequently.

An example of updating the replicas of the nginx deployment created declaratively is:

```
kubectl scale deployment nginx --replicas=5
```

This command scales up the "nginx" deployment to five replicas.

3.18 What are Taints and Tolerations in Kubernetes, and how do they help in scheduling Pods on Nodes?

In Kubernetes, Taints and Tolerations are used to control which Pods can be scheduled on which Nodes.

Taints

A Taint is a label applied to a Node that repels Pods. When a Node is tainted, it will not accept Pods that do not tolerate the taint. A Taint is specified by a key-value pair and a taint effect. The taint effect can be either NoSchedule, PreferNoSchedule, or NoExecute. The NoSchedule effect prevents new Pods from being scheduled on the tainted Node, the PreferNoSchedule effect tries to avoid scheduling new Pods on the tainted Node, and the NoExecute effect evicts existing Pods that do not tolerate the taint.

An example of tainting a Node is:

```
kubectl taint nodes node-1 app=nginx:NoSchedule
```

This command applies a taint to the Node named "node-1" with the key-value pair "app=nginx" and the effect "NoSchedule". This means that any Pod without a corresponding toleration for this taint will not be scheduled on this Node.

Tolerations

A Toleration is a property applied to a Pod that allows it to tolerate a taint. When a Pod has a toleration for a specific taint, it can be scheduled on the tainted Node. A Toleration is specified by a key-value pair and an effect that matches the corresponding taint.

An example of adding a toleration to a Pod is:

```
apiVersion: v1
kind: Pod
metadata:
  name: nginx-pod
spec:
  containers:
  - name: nginx
    image: nginx:latest
  tolerations:
  - key: app
    operator: Equal
    value: nginx
    effect: NoSchedule
```

This YAML file specifies a Pod named "nginx-pod" with an Nginx container. The toleration allows the Pod to be scheduled on a Node with a taint that has the key-value pair "app=nginx" and the effect "NoSchedule".

Taints and Tolerations are useful in Kubernetes cluster setups where specific Nodes have special hardware or are dedicated to certain workloads. They ensure that Pods are scheduled on Nodes that meet specific requirements, helping to optimize resource utilization and ensure high availability of applications.

3.19 Discuss the role of Kubernetes Custom Resource Definitions (CRDs).

Kubernetes Custom Resource Definitions (CRDs) allow users to define and use their custom resources within a Kubernetes cluster. They provide a way to extend the Kubernetes API to support new types of resources beyond the built-in types such as Pods, Services, and Deployments. CRDs are a powerful feature that enables users to define their own application-specific objects in Kubernetes and use them just like any other Kubernetes resource.

To define a CRD, you create a custom resource definition object in Kubernetes. This object contains a description of the new resource type, including its name, version, and schema. The schema defines the structure of the resource and the allowed fields, as well as any default values and validation rules.

Here's an example of a CRD that defines a custom resource called "Foo" with two fields: "name" and "size":

```
apiVersion: apiextensions.k8s.io/v1
kind: CustomResourceDefinition
metadata:
  name: foos.example.com
spec:
  group: example.com
  version: v1alpha1
  scope: Namespaced
  names:
    plural: foos
    singular: foo
    kind: Foo
  validation:
    openAPIV3Schema:
      type: object
      properties:
        name:
          type: string
        size:
          type: integer
```

Once you have defined a CRD, you can create instances of the new resource type in the same way as other Kubernetes resources. For

example, to create an instance of the "Foo" resource defined above,
you would use a YAML manifest like this:

```
apiVersion: example.com/v1alpha1
kind: Foo
metadata:
  name: my-foo
spec:
  name: bar
  size: 42
```

CRDs are useful in a variety of scenarios, such as when you need
to define custom resources to manage stateful applications or spe-
cialized hardware resources. They provide a simple and consistent
way to extend Kubernetes to support new types of resources and
enable users to easily manage their applications and infrastructure.

3.20 Describe the process of securing container images in a Kubernetes environment.

Securing container images in a Kubernetes environment is an important aspect of ensuring the overall security of the cluster. Here
are some best practices and steps that can be followed to secure
container images:

Use secure base images: Start with a base image that has a good
reputation for security and is regularly updated with the latest
security patches.

Scan container images for vulnerabilities: Use a container image
scanner tool such as Clair, Trivy, or Anchore to scan container
images for known vulnerabilities and other security issues.

Use signed images: Use signed container images to ensure that the
images you are using are from a trusted source and have not been
tampered with.

Implement Role-Based Access Control (RBAC): Use RBAC to restrict access to Kubernetes resources and ensure that only authorized users can access and deploy container images.

Use Secrets for storing sensitive data: Use Kubernetes Secrets to store sensitive data such as passwords, API keys, and other secrets needed to run applications within the cluster.

Implement network security policies: Use Kubernetes network policies to restrict network traffic between containers and limit exposure to potential security threats.

Implement Pod Security Policies: Use Pod Security Policies to define security requirements for pods, such as what user or group a container can run as or whether a container can mount a host file system.

Here are some example commands and configurations that can be used to implement some of these security measures:

To scan container images for vulnerabilities using Trivy:

```
trivy image <image\_name>
```

To implement Role-Based Access Control (RBAC) in Kubernetes:

```
kubectl create role <role\_name> --verb=<verb> --resource=<resource>
    --namespace=<namespace>
kubectl create rolebinding <role\_binding\_name> --role=<role\_name>
    --user=<user> --namespace=<namespace>
```

To use Kubernetes Secrets to store sensitive data:

```
kubectl create secret generic <secret\_name> --from-literal=<key>=<
    value>
```

To implement a network policy:

```
apiVersion: networking.k8s.io/v1
kind: NetworkPolicy
metadata:
  name: deny-all
spec:
  podSelector: {}
  policyTypes:
  - Ingress
  - Egress
  ingress: []
  egress: []
```

To implement a Pod Security Policy:

```
apiVersion: policy/v1beta1
kind: PodSecurityPolicy
metadata:
```

```
  name: restrictive-psp
spec:
  privileged: false
  seLinux:
    rule: RunAsAny
  runAsUser:
    rule: MustRunAsNonRoot
  fsGroup:
    rule: RunAsAny
  volumes:
  - '*'
```

Overall, securing container images in a Kubernetes environment requires a combination of best practices, tools, and configurations. By following these steps, you can help ensure the security of your Kubernetes cluster and the applications running within it.

Chapter 4

Advanced

4.1 Describe the Kubernetes control plane and its components, including the API server, etcd, controller manager, and scheduler.

The Kubernetes control plane is the set of components that manage and control the Kubernetes cluster. It includes several key components that work together to provide a cohesive and robust environment for managing containerized applications.

One of the most important components of the control plane is the Kubernetes API server. This server provides a central point of access for all Kubernetes operations and management tasks, allowing administrators and developers to interact with the cluster and its resources through a unified API. The API server also serves as the gateway for all communication between the various components of the control plane and the worker nodes.

Another key component of the control plane is etcd, which serves as the distributed database that stores the configuration data and state of the Kubernetes cluster. All of the resources in the cluster are represented as objects in etcd, and changes to these objects are communicated through the API server. Etcd ensures that the state of the cluster remains consistent and up-to-date across all nodes, even in the face of failures or network partitions.

The Kubernetes controller manager is responsible for monitoring the state of the cluster and ensuring that the desired state is maintained. It does this by continuously monitoring the objects in etcd and taking actions to reconcile any differences between the desired state and the actual state of the cluster. For example, if a Pod fails or is deleted, the controller manager will automatically create a new Pod to replace it.

Finally, the scheduler is responsible for determining which worker node a new Pod should be scheduled on. It does this by evaluating a variety of factors, such as the resource requirements of the Pod and the available resources on each node, and making an informed decision about where to place the Pod.

Together, these components form the core of the Kubernetes control plane, providing the necessary infrastructure for managing and orchestrating containerized applications in a distributed environment.

4.2 Explain the role of the Kubernetes API server in the control plane.

The Kubernetes API server is a central component of the Kubernetes control plane. It acts as the front-end interface for managing the Kubernetes cluster and provides a RESTful API for Kubernetes objects and services. The API server accepts requests from various sources such as kubectl, controllers, and other components within the control plane.

The API server is responsible for authentication and authorization of client requests, ensuring that only authorized users can access the cluster. It also serves as a gateway to other Kubernetes components, including etcd, the controller manager, and the scheduler.

The API server stores the state of the Kubernetes cluster by using etcd, a highly available distributed key-value store. It keeps track of the desired state of Kubernetes objects and services, and it continuously reconciles the current state with the desired state.

The API server also handles validation of Kubernetes objects and services by checking them against the Kubernetes API schema. It enforces access control policies, such as role-based access control (RBAC), by authorizing requests based on the permissions of the user or service account making the request.

To interact with the Kubernetes API server, you can use the kubectl command-line tool, which sends HTTP requests to the API server. You can also interact with the API server using client libraries in various programming languages, including Go, Python, Java, and others.

Here is an example command to retrieve the Kubernetes API server endpoint:

```
kubectl cluster-info
```

This will display information about the Kubernetes cluster, including the API server endpoint.

4.3 What is a StatefulSet and how does it differ from a Deployment in managing stateful applications?

In Kubernetes, a StatefulSet is a controller object used for managing stateful applications. It is similar to a Deployment in that it manages a set of replicated Pods, but it is designed specifically for applications that require stable, unique network identities and persistent storage. This is particularly useful for stateful applications such as databases or message brokers that require stable hostnames or storage volumes.

Unlike Deployments, StatefulSets guarantee a unique identity and stable hostname for each Pod they manage. This is achieved by using a stable network identity for each Pod based on its ordinal index. For example, if a StatefulSet is managing three replicas, the first Pod will have a stable hostname of pod-0, the second will have a hostname of pod-1, and so on. This allows stateful applications to be deployed and scaled while maintaining consistent network identities.

Another key difference between StatefulSets and Deployments is in how they manage persistent storage. Deployments assume that their Pods are stateless and can be terminated and replaced at any time without loss of data. StatefulSets, on the other hand, assume that their Pods are stateful and require persistent storage to maintain data. As a result, each Pod in a StatefulSet is assigned a unique persistent volume claim (PVC) that is not deleted when the Pod is terminated.

Overall, StatefulSets are a powerful tool for managing stateful applications in Kubernetes, providing stable network identities and persistent storage. However, they are more complex to manage than Deployments and require careful consideration of the underlying infrastructure and application requirements.

Example:

Here is an example of a simple StatefulSet definition for running a stateful application such as a database:

```
apiVersion: apps/v1
kind: StatefulSet
metadata:
  name: db
spec:
  selector:
    matchLabels:
      app: db
  serviceName: "db"
  replicas: 3
  template:
    metadata:
      labels:
        app: db
    spec:
      containers:
      - name: db
        image: mydb:latest
        ports:
        - containerPort: 5432
        volumeMounts:
        - name: data
          mountPath: /var/lib/postgresql/data
  volumeClaimTemplates:
  - metadata:
      name: data
    spec:
      accessModes: [ "ReadWriteOnce" ]
      resources:
```

```
requests:
    storage: 1Gi
```

In this example, the StatefulSet manages a set of three replicas of a database container. Each replica is assigned a unique network identity based on its ordinal index (db-0, db-1, db-2). The container is configured with a persistent volume mount at /var/lib/postgresql/-data using a volume claim template that ensures each replica has its own unique storage volume.

4.4 Describe the process of setting up High Availability (HA) in a Kubernetes cluster.

Setting up High Availability (HA) in a Kubernetes cluster is an essential aspect of ensuring that the cluster is resilient and can withstand failures. In this process, multiple instances of each control plane component are set up in different nodes, making sure that the cluster can still function even if one of the nodes goes down.

Here are the steps involved in setting up High Availability in a Kubernetes cluster:

Set up a load balancer: A load balancer is required to distribute traffic evenly among the control plane nodes. A popular choice for Kubernetes is the cloud load balancer service or an on-premises load balancer solution like HAProxy.

Set up multiple control plane nodes: At least three control plane nodes should be set up for High Availability. Each node will have a copy of the Kubernetes API server, etcd, and other control plane components. The number of nodes required may vary depending on the size of the cluster and its expected workload.

Configure the etcd cluster: Etcd is a distributed key-value store used by Kubernetes to store configuration data. Etcd needs to be set up as a cluster with multiple nodes, ensuring that data is replicated across all nodes.

Install and configure control plane components: Kubernetes control plane components such as the API server, etcd, controller manager, and scheduler should be installed and configured on each control plane node.

Verify the setup: Verify the setup by testing the Kubernetes cluster for failover scenarios, ensuring that it can handle the loss of a control plane node without any downtime.

Here is an example command to create a three-node control plane cluster:

```
kubeadm init --control-plane-endpoint=<LOAD_BALANCER_IP>
   --upload-certs --apiserver-advertise-address=<
       CONTROL_PLANE_NODE_IP>
   --apiserver-cert-extra-sans=<LOAD_BALANCER_DNS>
```

In the above command, the –control-plane-endpoint option specifies the IP address of the load balancer, and the –apiserver-advertise-address option specifies the IP address of the current control plane node.

Once the cluster is set up, you can use the kubectl get nodes command to verify that all nodes are running and ready.

Overall, setting up High Availability in a Kubernetes cluster involves ensuring that multiple copies of control plane components are set up across different nodes, with each node configured to handle traffic and data in a resilient manner. This helps to ensure that the cluster can function even in the event of node failures or other issues.

4.5 Explain how Kubernetes handles persistent storage using Persistent Volumes (PV), Persistent Volume Claims (PVC), and Storage Classes.

Kubernetes provides a flexible and extensible architecture for handling persistent storage. Persistent Volumes (PVs) represent a physical storage resource in a cluster, while Persistent Volume Claims (PVCs) are used by applications to request a specific amount of storage from the cluster. Storage Classes provide a way to dynamically provision PVs based on different parameters, such as performance, availability, or cost.

Here is a step-by-step explanation of how persistent storage is handled in Kubernetes:

Create a Storage Class: A Storage Class defines the underlying storage provider and the parameters for dynamically provisioning Persistent Volumes. For example, a Storage Class can specify a specific storage provider like AWS EBS or Google Cloud Storage, as well as the performance and redundancy characteristics of the storage.

```
kind: StorageClass
apiVersion: storage.k8s.io/v1
metadata:
  name: fast
provisioner: kubernetes.io/aws-ebs
parameters:
  type: gp2
```

Create a Persistent Volume Claim: A Persistent Volume Claim is a request for storage from a Kubernetes cluster. A PVC can specify the amount of storage needed, as well as the Storage Class to use for provisioning the Persistent Volume.

```
kind: PersistentVolumeClaim
apiVersion: v1
metadata:
  name: my-claim
spec:
  accessModes:
    - ReadWriteOnce
  resources:
    requests:
      storage: 10Gi
  storageClassName: fast
```

Bind a Persistent Volume to a Persistent Volume Claim: Once a PVC is created, Kubernetes will automatically provision a new PV that satisfies the request. The PV is then bound to the PVC, allowing the application to use the requested storage.

```
kind: PersistentVolumeClaim
apiVersion: v1
metadata:
  name: my-claim
spec:
  accessModes:
    - ReadWriteOnce
  resources:
```

```
    requests:
       storage: 10Gi
    storageClassName: fast
    volumeName: my-pv
```

Mount the Persistent Volume in a Pod: The final step is to mount the PV in a Pod. The Pod can use the Persistent Volume as a regular file system, and any data written to the mount point will be stored in the underlying storage provider.

```
apiVersion: v1
kind: Pod
metadata:
  name: my-pod
spec:
  containers:
    - name: my-container
      image: nginx
      volumeMounts:
        - name: my-volume
          mountPath: /var/www/html
  volumes:
    - name: my-volume
      persistentVolumeClaim:
        claimName: my-claim
```

Persistent storage in Kubernetes is a powerful feature that allows applications to store and access data in a scalable and reliable way. By using PVs, PVCs, and Storage Classes, Kubernetes provides a unified interface for managing storage across different cloud providers and storage systems.

4.6 What are Kubernetes Operators, and how do they extend the functionality of the platform?

Kubernetes Operators are software extensions to Kubernetes that automate the management of complex applications or services. They are built on top of the Kubernetes API and use custom resources to define and manage the state of applications.

Operators are designed to extend the functionality of Kubernetes beyond its core features. They enable users to create custom controllers that automate the deployment and management of complex applications, databases, and other stateful services. By leveraging the Kubernetes API and resource model, Operators can provide a consistent way of deploying and managing applications, regardless of the underlying infrastructure.

Operators are built using a set of APIs and tools provided by the Kubernetes Operator Framework. This framework provides a set of best practices and reusable components for building Operators. It includes tools for generating code, testing, and deploying Operators.

To create an Operator, you first need to define a custom resource definition (CRD) that defines the desired state of your application. The CRD specifies the schema for the custom resource, which includes the fields and validation rules for the resource. You can then use this CRD to define a custom controller that watches for changes to the resource and takes actions to ensure the application is running as desired.

For example, a MySQL Operator might define a custom resource for a MySQL database that includes the desired number of replicas, storage requirements, and other configuration options. The custom controller would then monitor this resource and take actions to ensure the correct number of replicas are running, storage is provisioned, and the database is configured correctly.

Operators can be used to automate the management of a wide range of applications and services, including databases, message brokers, and other stateful services. They can also be used to simplify the deployment and management of complex applications that require multiple containers or services.

Some popular examples of Operators include the Prometheus Operator for managing the Prometheus monitoring system, the etcd Operator for managing the etcd distributed key-value store, and the Kafka Operator for managing the Apache Kafka messaging system.

Overall, Kubernetes Operators provide a powerful mechanism for extending the functionality of Kubernetes and simplifying the management of complex applications and services.

4.7 Discuss the key security features in Kubernetes, such as Role-Based Access Control (RBAC), Network Policies, and Pod Security Policies (PSP).

Kubernetes provides several security features to ensure the safety and security of the cluster, such as Role-Based Access Control (RBAC), Network Policies, and Pod Security Policies (PSP).

Role-Based Access Control (RBAC): RBAC is a method of regulating access to resources in a Kubernetes cluster. It allows administrators to define specific roles and permissions for users and groups within the cluster. Roles can be defined for specific namespaces or for the entire cluster. Users can be granted different levels of access, such as read-only, read-write, or full control. RBAC also allows for easy management of access permissions, as roles and users can be easily added, modified, or removed.

To create a RoleBinding that grants a user read-only access to a specific namespace, we can use the following example YAML:

```
apiVersion: rbac.authorization.k8s.io/v1
kind: RoleBinding
metadata:
  name: read-only-access
  namespace: my-namespace
subjects:
- kind: User
  name: john
  apiGroup: rbac.authorization.k8s.io
roleRef:
  kind: Role
  name: read-only-role
  apiGroup: rbac.authorization.k8s.io
```

This RoleBinding grants user "john" read-only access to the "my-namespace" namespace using the "read-only-role" Role.

Network Policies: Network Policies in Kubernetes are used to control the network traffic flow between Pods and/or from external sources. They define rules that allow or deny traffic based on various criteria such as source and destination IP addresses, ports, and protocols. Network Policies can be defined for specific Pods or for entire namespaces.

To create a Network Policy that allows traffic only from a specific IP address range to a set of Pods, we can use the following example YAML:

```
apiVersion: networking.k8s.io/v1
kind: NetworkPolicy
metadata:
  name: allow-from-ip-range
  namespace: my-namespace
spec:
  podSelector:
    matchLabels:
      app: my-app
  policyTypes:
  - Ingress
  ingress:
  - from:
    - ipBlock:
        cidr: 10.0.0.0/8
    ports:
    - protocol: TCP
      port: 80
```

This Network Policy allows traffic only from the IP address range "10.0.0.0/8" to Pods with the label "app=my-app" in the "my-namespace" namespace on port 80.

Pod Security Policies (PSP): Pod Security Policies are used to restrict the actions that can be performed by Pods within a Kubernetes cluster. They define a set of security constraints that must be met before a Pod can be scheduled to run. PSPs can be used to limit the use of privileged containers, restrict the use of host namespaces and devices, and control the use of security contexts.

To create a Pod Security Policy that restricts the use of privileged containers, we can use the following example YAML:

```
apiVersion: policy/v1beta1
kind: PodSecurityPolicy
metadata:
  name: restrict-privileged-containers
spec:
  privileged: false
  allowPrivilegeEscalation: false
  allowedCapabilities:
  - "NET\_ADMIN"
  - "SYS\_TIME"
  seLinux:
    rule: RunAsAny
  supplementalGroups:
    rule: RunAsAny
  fsGroup:
    rule: RunAsAny
  runAsUser:
    rule: RunAsAny
```

This Pod Security Policy restricts the use of privileged containers by setting "privileged" and "allowPrivilegeEscalation" to false. It also allows only the "NET_ADMIN"

4.8 Describe the Kubernetes networking model, including the role of the Container Network Interface (CNI) and the use of network plugins.

Kubernetes networking model provides a flat network that enables communication between all the pods in the cluster. It is an essential component that enables different services, containers, and applications to communicate with each other seamlessly. In Kubernetes, the networking model provides a way to communicate between different nodes in the cluster as well as the pods that are running on them.

The Container Network Interface (CNI) is an interface that Kubernetes uses to configure the network of the nodes and the pods running on them. The CNI plugin is responsible for creating a virtual network interface that enables communication between the different pods running in the cluster.

Kubernetes uses network plugins to implement the CNI specification. These plugins provide different networking capabilities, such as network isolation, IP allocation, and load balancing. Some of the commonly used network plugins include Calico, Flannel, Canal, Weave Net, and Cilium. Each network plugin has its own set of features and capabilities, so it is essential to choose the right plugin based on your specific requirements.

Role-Based Access Control (RBAC) is a security feature in Kubernetes that enables administrators to control who can access and modify different resources in the cluster. RBAC can be used to grant or deny permissions to individual users, groups of users, or service accounts. This feature helps ensure that only authorized users have access to sensitive resources in the cluster.

Network Policies are another security feature in Kubernetes that enable administrators to control the flow of network traffic between different pods in the cluster. Network Policies can be used to define rules that specify which pods can communicate with each other and which protocols and ports are allowed. This feature helps ensure that only authorized traffic is allowed between different pods in the cluster.

Pod Security Policies (PSP) is another security feature in Kubernetes that enables administrators to control the security context of pods running in the cluster. PSP can be used to define policies that specify the privileges and capabilities that are available to different pods. This feature helps ensure that the pods running in the cluster are secure and cannot be used to compromise the overall security of the cluster.

Example of creating a Network Policy in Kubernetes:

```
apiVersion: networking.k8s.io/v1
kind: NetworkPolicy
metadata:
  name: allow-nginx-to-db
spec:
  podSelector:
    matchLabels:
      app: db
  policyTypes:
  - Ingress
  ingress:
  - from:
    - podSelector:
        matchLabels:
          app: nginx
    ports:
    - protocol: TCP
      port: 3306
```

This Network Policy specifies that the pods labeled with app: db can only receive incoming traffic from pods labeled with app: nginx on port 3306.

4.9 What are Custom Resource Definitions (CRDs) in Kubernetes, and how do they enable extensibility?

Custom Resource Definitions (CRDs) are one of the advanced features of Kubernetes that enable the platform to be extended beyond the built-in resources. They allow developers to create their own custom resources and manage them using Kubernetes' declarative API.

CRDs essentially define a new object kind, which can be treated as a first-class Kubernetes object in the same way as Pods, Deployments, and Services. They can be used to create a higher-level abstraction on top of the built-in resources or to introduce new resource types that are specific to an application or domain.

To create a CRD, you need to define a new API resource in Kubernetes. This can be done using a YAML or JSON file that specifies the resource's schema, behavior, and metadata. Here is an example YAML file that defines a CRD for a custom resource named MyResource:

```
apiVersion: apiextensions.k8s.io/v1beta1
kind: CustomResourceDefinition
metadata:
  name: myresources.example.com
spec:
  group: example.com
  version: v1
  scope: Namespaced
  names:
    plural: myresources
    singular: myresource
    kind: MyResource
    shortNames:
    - mr
  validation:
    openAPIV3Schema:
      type: object
      properties:
        name:
          type: string
        value:
          type: integer
      required:
      - name
      - value
```

In this example, the CustomResourceDefinition object defines a

new API resource named MyResource, which belongs to the exam-
ple.com group and the v1 version. The scope field specifies that
this resource is namespaced, meaning it can only be used within a
specific namespace. The names field specifies the plural and sin-
gular names of the resource, as well as a shorthand name. The
validation field specifies the schema for the resource's data, which
in this case includes a required name field and an optional value
field.

Once the CRD is defined, you can use it to create instances of the
custom resource using the Kubernetes API. For example, here is
a YAML file that creates an instance of the MyResource custom
resource:

```
apiVersion: example.com/v1
kind: MyResource
metadata:
  name: my-resource-1
spec:
  name: example
  value: 42
```

This YAML file creates a new instance of the MyResource custom
resource with the name my-resource-1, and sets the name field to
"example" and the value field to 42.

CRDs are powerful because they allow developers to create custom
resources that can be managed using the same Kubernetes tools
and APIs as the built-in resources. This makes it easy to integrate
custom resources with other Kubernetes objects and to automate
management tasks using tools like Kubernetes Operators. CRDs
also enable better observability and automation by defining the
desired state of an application or system as a declarative resource,
which can be version-controlled and audited.

4.10 Explain how Kubernetes handles container logging and monitoring, including the role of Prometheus, Grafana, and Fluentd.

Kubernetes provides a flexible logging and monitoring system that allows you to collect and analyze data from your cluster's resources, including Pods, Nodes, and containers. The platform supports a range of popular logging and monitoring tools, including Prometheus, Grafana, and Fluentd.

Logging in Kubernetes

Kubernetes provides two primary methods for container logging: stdout and stderr. By default, Kubernetes captures these logs and forwards them to the platform's logging system, which is implemented using the Fluentd log collector. Fluentd is responsible for routing and filtering logs, and it can send them to a variety of destinations, including Elasticsearch, Kafka, and syslog servers.

You can customize Kubernetes logging by configuring the logging driver for each container in a Pod. For example, you can configure a container to send its logs to a specific file, to the system log, or to a remote syslog server. Here's an example of a Pod definition that sets the logging driver for a container:

```
apiVersion: v1
kind: Pod
metadata:
  name: my-pod
spec:
  containers:
  - name: my-container
    image: my-image
    args: ["echo", "hello world"]
    resources:
      limits:
        memory: "512Mi"
        cpu: "500m"
    logging:
      driver: syslog
      options:
        syslog-address: "tcp://my-syslog-server:514"
```

In this example, the logging section specifies that the container should use the syslog logging driver and send logs to the my-syslog-server server on port 514.

Monitoring in Kubernetes

Kubernetes provides a range of built-in monitoring features that allow you to track and analyze the health of your cluster and its resources. These features include:

Kubernetes API Server: The API server provides a comprehensive view of the state of the cluster, including information on Nodes, Pods, and other resources.

Kubernetes Metrics Server: The Metrics Server collects metrics data from Nodes and Pods, including CPU usage, memory usage, and network bandwidth. This data is stored in the Kubernetes API server and can be accessed by monitoring tools like Prometheus.

Prometheus: Prometheus is an open-source monitoring system that is widely used in the Kubernetes ecosystem. It allows you to collect and analyze time-series data, including metrics from the Kubernetes Metrics Server.

Grafana: Grafana is a popular open-source dashboarding tool that is used to visualize and analyze data from Prometheus and other data sources. It provides a range of built-in dashboards for Kubernetes monitoring, including views of CPU and memory usage, network traffic, and application performance.

To set up monitoring in Kubernetes, you can follow these general steps:

Install the Kubernetes Metrics Server: The Metrics Server is a core component of Kubernetes monitoring, and it provides a rich set of metrics data that can be used by monitoring tools like Prometheus. You can install the Metrics Server using a YAML file:

```
kubectl apply -f https://github.com/kubernetes-sigs/metrics-server/
    releases/latest/download/components.yaml
```

Install Prometheus: Prometheus can be installed using a Helm chart or by deploying it directly using a YAML file. Once installed, you'll need to configure Prometheus to scrape metrics data from the Kubernetes Metrics Server.

Install Grafana: Grafana can be installed using a Helm chart or by deploying it directly using a YAML file. Once installed, you can connect it to your Prometheus instance to create dashboards and visualize your monitoring data.

Configure alerts: You can use Prometheus to define alerting rules that trigger notifications when certain conditions are met, such as high CPU usage or low disk space.

Overall, Kubernetes provides a powerful logging and monitoring system that allows you to collect,

4.11 Describe the process of setting up a private container registry and integrating it with a Kubernetes cluster.

Setting up a private container registry and integrating it with a Kubernetes cluster is a common task when working with Kubernetes. This allows developers to store and share their container images securely within their organization or team. In this answer, we will discuss the process of setting up a private container registry and integrating it with a Kubernetes cluster.

There are several popular container registry solutions, such as Docker Hub, Google Container Registry, and Amazon Elastic Container Registry. However, for this answer, we will use Docker Registry as an example since it is an open-source solution that can be installed on-premises.

Here are the steps to set up a private Docker Registry and integrate it with a Kubernetes cluster:

Install Docker Registry on-premises

First, we need to install Docker Registry on-premises. This can be done using the following command:

```
\$ docker run -d -p 5000:5000 --restart=always --name registry
    registry:2
```

This command will start a Docker Registry container on port 5000 with automatic restarts and the name "registry". Note that this is a basic example, and you may need to customize the configuration based on your specific requirements.

Secure the Docker Registry

By default, the Docker Registry is not secured, and anyone with access to the server can push and pull images. To secure the Docker Registry, we need to set up TLS encryption and authentication.

To set up TLS encryption, we need to generate a self-signed certificate and key:

```
\$ openssl req -newkey rsa:4096 -nodes -sha256 -keyout domain.key -
    x509 -days 365 -out domain.crt
```

Then, we need to modify the Docker Registry configuration file to use the certificate and key:

```
vi /etc/docker/registry/config.yml
```

Add the following lines to the file:

```
tls:
  certificate: /etc/docker/certs/domain.crt
  key: /etc/docker/certs/domain.key
```

To set up authentication, we can use basic authentication or token authentication. For basic authentication, we can create a "htpasswd" file containing username and password pairs:

```
\$ htpasswd -Bbn username password > /path/to/htpasswd
```

Then, we need to modify the Docker Registry configuration file to use the "htpasswd" file:

```
auth:
  htpasswd:
    realm: basic-realm
    path: /path/to/htpasswd
```

Test the Docker Registry

After securing the Docker Registry, we can test it by pushing and pulling images:

```
\$ docker tag nginx localhost:5000/nginx
\$ docker push localhost:5000/nginx
\$ docker pull localhost:5000/nginx
```

Configure the Kubernetes cluster

To integrate the private Docker Registry with a Kubernetes cluster, we need to configure the cluster to use the registry as an image repository.

First, we need to create a Kubernetes Secret to store the authentication credentials:

```
\$ kubectl create secret docker-registry regcred --docker-server=
    localhost:5000 --docker-username=username --docker-password=
    password --docker-email=email@example.com
```

Then, we need to create a Kubernetes deployment that uses the private Docker Registry as the image repository:

```
apiVersion: apps/v1
kind: Deployment
metadata:
  name: myapp
spec:
  replicas: 1
  selector:
    matchLabels:
      app: myapp
  template:
    metadata:
      labels:
        app: myapp
    spec:
      containers:
        - name: myapp
          image: localhost:5000/myimage
      imagePullSecrets:
        - name: regcred
```

4.12 Explain how Kubernetes manages container image security, including image scanning and using a trusted base image.

Kubernetes offers several features to manage container image security, including image scanning and the use of trusted base images.

One of the most important aspects of container image security is ensuring that images used in a Kubernetes cluster are free from known vulnerabilities. Image scanning is a process of analyzing the contents of a container image for known security vulnerabilities, which can help identify and mitigate potential security threats. Kubernetes can be integrated with image scanning tools like Aqua Security, Anchore, and Clair to scan container images for known vulnerabilities.

Kubernetes also offers the ability to use trusted base images. A trusted base image is a base image that has been pre-configured with security settings and has been tested and validated by the organization. By using a trusted base image, organizations can reduce the risk of security vulnerabilities in their container images.

To use a trusted base image in Kubernetes, a developer can specify the base image in the Dockerfile or Kubernetes manifest file, or use a container image scanner to verify that the image has been built with a trusted base image. Additionally, Kubernetes can be configured to enforce policies that ensure only approved images are used in the cluster.

Example:

```
\# Dockerfile using a trusted base image
FROM myorg/trusted-base-image:latest
COPY app.py .
CMD ["python", "app.py"]
```

Kubernetes can also integrate with other security tools such as vulnerability scanners, runtime security tools, and network security tools to provide a comprehensive security framework for containerized applications. Overall, Kubernetes provides several features and integrations to manage container image security and ensure the security of containerized applications running in a cluster.

4.13 Discuss the role of service meshes, such as Istio or Linkerd, in a Kubernetes environment and their advantages.

Service meshes are a layer of infrastructure that is deployed in a Kubernetes environment to manage the communication between microservices. They provide a way to control and monitor network traffic, as well as implement features such as load balancing, service discovery, and security. Two popular service meshes for Kubernetes are Istio and Linkerd.

Istio is a service mesh that provides a way to connect, secure, and monitor microservices. It has features such as traffic management, security, and observability. Istio uses Envoy as a sidecar proxy to intercept and manage network traffic between microservices. Istio also provides a control plane that allows operators to configure policies and rules for microservices.

Linkerd is a service mesh that focuses on simplicity and reliability. It provides features such as traffic management, security, and observability. Linkerd uses a lightweight proxy to intercept and manage network traffic between microservices. Linkerd also provides a control plane that allows operators to configure policies and rules for microservices.

Some advantages of using a service mesh in a Kubernetes environment include:

Traffic management: A service mesh provides features such as load balancing and routing that can help distribute network traffic to different microservices.

Security: Service meshes provide features such as authentication and encryption that can help secure communication between microservices.

Observability: Service meshes provide features such as monitoring and tracing that can help operators understand the behavior of microservices and troubleshoot issues.

To install Istio in a Kubernetes environment, you can use the following steps:

Download and install the Istio command-line interface (CLI).

Use the CLI to install Istio in your Kubernetes cluster.

Deploy your microservices and configure Istio to manage the traffic between them.

To install Linkerd in a Kubernetes environment, you can use the following steps:

Download and install the Linkerd command-line interface (CLI).

Use the CLI to install Linkerd in your Kubernetes cluster.

Deploy your microservices and configure Linkerd to manage the traffic between them.

Example code:

To install Istio in a Kubernetes cluster using the command-line interface, you can use the following command:

```
istioctl install --set profile=default
```

This command installs Istio in the default profile, which includes the core features of Istio such as traffic management, security, and observability.

To install Linkerd in a Kubernetes cluster using the command-line interface, you can use the following command:

```
linkerd install | kubectl apply -f -
```

This command installs Linkerd in your Kubernetes cluster and deploys the necessary components to manage network traffic between microservices.

4.14 Explain the concept of GitOps and how it can be applied to manage Kubernetes deployments.

GitOps is a methodology for managing the deployment of applications and infrastructure on Kubernetes, based on version control system (VCS) and Git workflows. It is a way to manage changes to Kubernetes resources, such as configurations and deployments, by committing them to a Git repository, where they can be versioned, reviewed, and audited. GitOps follows the principles of declarative infrastructure, where the desired state of the system is defined in configuration files, and the system automatically adjusts to the desired state.

The GitOps workflow typically involves a continuous delivery pipeline, which monitors the Git repository for changes and automatically deploys them to the Kubernetes cluster. This is done by using a GitOps tool, such as Flux or Argo CD, which acts as a controller for the cluster and synchronizes the desired state of the system with the Git repository.

The key advantages of GitOps are:

Versioning: By using Git as the source of truth, changes can be versioned and reviewed, providing greater transparency and auditability.

Reliability: By using a declarative approach, the desired state of the system is clearly defined, reducing the risk of errors and ensuring consistency across deployments.

Collaboration: By using Git workflows, multiple team members can collaborate on changes to the infrastructure, enabling a more efficient and scalable process.

Scalability: By automating the deployment process, GitOps allows for more frequent and reliable deployments, enabling faster iterations and better scalability.

Example of a GitOps workflow:

Developers make changes to the configuration files in their local Git repository.

They commit and push the changes to the central Git repository.

A GitOps tool, such as Flux or Argo CD, monitors the Git repository for changes.

When changes are detected, the GitOps tool applies the changes to the Kubernetes cluster.

The state of the system is reconciled with the Git repository, ensuring that the desired state is always maintained.

Here is an example of how to set up a GitOps pipeline using Flux:

Install Flux in the Kubernetes cluster using the following command:

```
kubectl apply -f https://raw.githubusercontent.com/fluxcd/flux/main/
    install.yaml
```

Set up a Git repository for the configuration files and add a deployment key to the repository.

Create a Flux configuration file, such as the following example:

```
apiVersion: source.toolkit.fluxcd.io/v1beta1
kind: GitRepository
metadata:
  name: example
spec:
  interval: 1m
  url: git@github.com:example/repository.git
  ref:
    branch: main
---
apiVersion: kustomize.toolkit.fluxcd.io/v1beta1
kind: Kustomization
metadata:
  name: example
spec:
  interval: 1m
  path: ./kustomize
```

Create a Kustomize directory with the configuration files for the application.

Commit and push the Flux configuration file and the Kustomize directory to the Git repository.

Flux will automatically detect the changes and apply the configuration to the Kubernetes cluster.

Monitor the GitOps pipeline and the state of the cluster using the Flux CLI or the Kubernetes dashboard.

In summary, GitOps is a powerful methodology for managing Kubernetes deployments, providing greater versioning, reliability, collaboration, and scalability. By using a GitOps tool, such as Flux or Argo CD, developers can automate the deployment process and ensure that the desired state of the system is always maintained.

4.15 What is a PodDisruptionBudget (PDB) in Kubernetes and how does it help maintain high availability during cluster maintenance?

A PodDisruptionBudget (PDB) is a Kubernetes object that helps to ensure the availability of a workload during disruptive events, such as maintenance or scaling operations, by defining constraints on the number of Pods that can be evicted from a ReplicaSet, Deployment, or StatefulSet at any given time.

PDBs are designed to work with the Kubernetes cluster's controller manager, which monitors the availability of resources in the cluster and ensures that the desired state is maintained. When a disruptive event occurs, such as a node maintenance or a pod eviction, the controller manager uses the PDBs to determine which Pods can be safely evicted without causing an outage.

To create a PodDisruptionBudget in Kubernetes, you can use a YAML or JSON manifest file, similar to other Kubernetes resources. Here is an example YAML manifest file for a PodDisruptionBudget:

```
apiVersion: policy/v1beta1
kind: PodDisruptionBudget
metadata:
  name: nginx-pdb
spec:
  minAvailable: 2
  selector:
```

```
matchLabels:
    app: nginx
```

In this example, the PodDisruptionBudget is named "nginx-pdb" and specifies that at least 2 Pods with the label "app: nginx" must be available at all times. If the number of available Pods falls below this threshold, the controller manager will block any further evictions until the desired state is restored.

PDBs are particularly useful in high availability scenarios where workload availability is critical, such as in production environments. By using PDBs, Kubernetes administrators can ensure that their applications remain available even during maintenance or scaling operations, reducing the risk of downtime and improving the overall reliability of the system.

4.16   Describe the process of implementing network segmentation and isolation using Kubernetes Network Policies.

Kubernetes Network Policies allow you to define rules to control the traffic flow between Pods in a Kubernetes cluster. By default, Pods can communicate with each other without restrictions. Network Policies provide a way to segment the network and isolate traffic between Pods in a more fine-grained manner.

To implement Network Policies in Kubernetes, you first need to ensure that your cluster supports it. This means that you must have a network plugin that implements the Kubernetes NetworkPolicy API. Many popular plugins like Calico, Weave Net, and Cilium support Network Policies out of the box.

Once you have a supported network plugin, you can start creating Network Policies to control the traffic flow. Network Policies are defined using YAML files and consist of one or more rules that specify which traffic should be allowed or denied. Each rule can match on various criteria such as the source or destination namespace, Pod labels, IP addresses, and ports.

Here is an example Network Policy that allows traffic only from a specific set of Pods:

```
apiVersion: networking.k8s.io/v1
kind: NetworkPolicy
metadata:
  name: allow-web-traffic
spec:
  podSelector:
    matchLabels:
      app: web
  ingress:
  - from:
    - podSelector:
        matchLabels:
          app: web
    - podSelector:
        matchLabels:
          app: db
    ports:
    - protocol: TCP
      port: 80
```

In this example, we have defined a Network Policy that allows traffic to Pods with the label app: web on port 80, but only from other Pods with the labels app: web or app: db. All other traffic is denied.

You can apply the Network Policy to your cluster using the kubectl apply command:

```
kubectl apply -f allow-web-traffic.yaml
```

Once the Network Policy is applied, you can verify its status using the kubectl describe command:

```
kubectl describe networkpolicy allow-web-traffic
```

Network Policies provide a powerful way to segment and isolate your Kubernetes network, but they require careful planning and testing to avoid unintended consequences. It's important to thoroughly understand how your applications communicate and to define policies that balance security and usability.

4.17 Explain how Kubernetes manages Secrets and ConfigMaps, and how they can be used to inject configuration data into applications.

Kubernetes provides two resources, Secrets and ConfigMaps, to store and manage configuration data that can be injected into containers as environment variables, command-line arguments, or mounted files.

Secrets in Kubernetes

Secrets are Kubernetes objects that store sensitive information, such as passwords, authentication tokens, or SSL certificates, in an encrypted form. Secrets can be created manually or generated from existing files using the kubectl create secret command. There are four types of Secrets:

generic: stores arbitrary key-value pairs

docker-registry: stores authentication credentials for a Docker registry

tls: stores a pair of SSL certificates and their private key

ssh: stores an SSH private key and its public key

Secrets are base64-encoded when stored, but they can be decoded when mounted into containers. Secrets can be mounted as environment variables or as files inside a container. To mount a Secret as an environment variable, define a container environment variable and set its value to the secret key, like this:

```
env:
- name: DB\_PASSWORD
  valueFrom:
    secretKeyRef:
      name: db-credentials
      key: password
```

To mount a Secret as a file, define a volume that references the Secret and mount the volume into the container, like this:

```
volumes:
```

```
- name: db-secrets
  secret:
    secretName: db-credentials
    items:
    - key: username
      path: db-username
    - key: password
      path: db-password
containers:
- name: app
  image: myapp:latest
  volumeMounts:
  - name: db-secrets
    mountPath: /etc/db-secrets
```

ConfigMaps in Kubernetes

ConfigMaps are Kubernetes objects that store non-sensitive config-uration data, such as configuration files, command-line arguments, or environment variables, in a key-value pair format. ConfigMaps can be created manually or generated from existing files or direc-tories using the kubectl create configmap command. ConfigMaps can be used in a similar way to Secrets, but they are not encrypted and can be used to store non-sensitive data.

ConfigMaps can be mounted as environment variables or as files inside a container. To mount a ConfigMap as an environment vari-able, define a container environment variable and set its value to the ConfigMap key, like this:

```
env:
- name: APP\_CONFIG
  valueFrom:
    configMapKeyRef:
      name: app-config
      key: config-file
```

To mount a ConfigMap as a file, define a volume that references the ConfigMap and mount the volume into the container, like this:

```
volumes:
- name: app-config
  configMap:
    name: app-config
containers:
- name: app
  image: myapp:latest
  volumeMounts:
  - name: app-config
    mountPath: /etc/app-config
```

Injecting Secrets and ConfigMaps into a Pod

Both Secrets and ConfigMaps can be injected into a Pod as environment variables or as files. To inject a Secret or a ConfigMap into a Pod as an environment variable, use the envFrom field and set its value to a list of secretRef or configMapRef objects, like this:

```
envFrom:
- secretRef:
    name: db-credentials
- configMapRef:
    name: app-config
```

To inject a Secret or a ConfigMap into a Pod as a file, define a volume that references the Secret or the ConfigMap and mount the volume into the container, like this:

```
volumes:
- name: db-secrets
  secret:
    secretName:
```

4.18 Discuss the role of admission controllers in Kubernetes and how they enhance security.

Admission controllers in Kubernetes are a powerful feature that provides a way to enforce policies and security mechanisms for objects that are being created, updated, or deleted in a cluster. Admission controllers intercept and modify API requests before they are persisted to the etcd data store, allowing administrators to enforce specific requirements on the objects created.

Admission controllers can be either mutating or validating. Mutating admission controllers modify the object in some way before it is persisted, while validating admission controllers only check that the object meets certain criteria.

There are many admission controllers available in Kubernetes, including the following:

PodSecurityPolicy: This admission controller validates that the Pod specification meets certain security policies. For example, it can ensure that the Pod runs as a non-root user, or that it doesn't mount sensitive host directories.

ResourceQuota: This admission controller enforces limits on the amount of resources (such as CPU and memory) that can be requested by a Pod or a Namespace.

NamespaceLifecycle: This admission controller ensures that only authorized users can create, update, or delete Namespaces.

DefaultStorageClass: This admission controller automatically sets a default StorageClass for a PersistentVolumeClaim if none is specified.

ImagePolicyWebhook: This admission controller checks that container images are signed by a trusted authority before they are pulled.

Admission controllers can be managed by modifying the kube-apiserver configuration file. For example, to enable the PodSecurityPolicy admission controller, the following line can be added to the configuration file:

```
--enable-admission-plugins=PodSecurityPolicy
```

Admission controllers play an important role in enhancing the security of a Kubernetes cluster, as they allow administrators to enforce specific policies and requirements on the objects created in the cluster. By using admission controllers, administrators can ensure that Pods and other objects are created with security in mind, and that they meet the requirements of the organization.

4.19 Explain the process of setting up and configuring a Kubernetes cluster from scratch.

Setting up and configuring a Kubernetes cluster from scratch involves several steps and can be a complex process, but here are the general steps:

Choose a cloud provider or set up your own hardware: Kubernetes can be run on a variety of cloud platforms, such as Google Cloud Platform, AWS, Azure, or you can set up your own infrastructure using bare-metal servers or virtual machines.

Install a container runtime: Kubernetes runs containerized applications, so you'll need to install a container runtime such as Docker or containerd on each node in your cluster.

Install and configure Kubernetes components: The Kubernetes control plane consists of several components, including the API server, etcd, kube-controller-manager, kube-scheduler, and kube-proxy. You'll need to install and configure these components on each node in your cluster.

Set up networking: Kubernetes requires a network overlay to facilitate communication between containers running on different nodes. Popular networking solutions include Calico, Flannel, and Weave Net.

Configure storage: Kubernetes supports several types of storage, including local storage, network-attached storage (NAS), and storage area network (SAN). You'll need to configure storage on each node in your cluster.

Set up authentication and authorization: Kubernetes provides several authentication and authorization mechanisms, including Role-Based Access Control (RBAC), Webhook, and OpenID Connect. You'll need to configure these mechanisms to control access to your cluster.

Install additional tools and plugins: There are several additional tools and plugins that can enhance the functionality of your Kubernetes cluster, such as Helm for package management, Prometheus for monitoring, and Istio for service mesh.

Here is an example of how to set up a Kubernetes cluster from scratch on a Google Cloud Platform:

Set up a Google Cloud Platform account and create a new project.

Install the Google Cloud SDK on your local machine.

Set up a Kubernetes cluster using the gcloud command-line tool:

```
gcloud container clusters create [CLUSTER\_NAME] --num-nodes [NUM\
    _NODES] --machine-type [MACHINE\_TYPE] --zone [ZONE]
```

Set up authentication and authorization using RBAC:

```
kubectl create clusterrolebinding cluster-admin-binding --
    clusterrole=cluster-admin --user=[USER\_ACCOUNT]
```

Set up networking using Calico:

```
kubectl apply -f https://docs.projectcalico.org/manifests/calico.
    yaml
```

Install additional tools and plugins, such as Helm:

```
curl https://raw.githubusercontent.com/helm/helm/main/scripts/get-
    helm-3 | bash
```

Configure storage using Persistent Volumes and Persistent Volume Claims.

Note that the exact steps and commands required to set up a Kubernetes cluster from scratch may vary depending on your specific environment and requirements.

4.20 Describe the role of Kubernetes Custom Controllers and how they can be used to automate and extend cluster functionality.

Kubernetes Custom Controllers are software components that extend the Kubernetes control plane by adding new behaviors and capabilities to the cluster. Custom Controllers can be created using the Kubernetes API and programming languages such as Go, Python, and Java.

Custom Controllers work by watching for specific events and changes in the Kubernetes API, such as the creation or deletion of resources, and then responding to those events by performing some action. Custom Controllers can be used to automate tasks, such as scaling applications or managing network policies, and to integrate with external systems and services.

Some common examples of Custom Controllers in Kubernetes include:

StatefulSet Controller: Manages stateful applications by ensuring
that each Pod has a unique hostname and persistent storage. DaemonSet Controller: Ensures that a specific Pod is running on each
node in the cluster, typically used for system-level tasks such as logging or monitoring. Job Controller: Runs a set of Pods to completion and then exits, typically used for batch processing or one-time
jobs. Operator Controller: Provides a higher level of abstraction
for managing complex applications, typically by using Custom Resources and Controllers specific to that application.

To create a Custom Controller, you would typically start by defining a Custom Resource Definition (CRD) that defines the new resource and its schema. You would then write a Controller that
watches for changes to that resource and takes action based on
those changes. The Controller would typically interact with the
Kubernetes API server to create, update, or delete other resources
as needed.

Here is an example of a simple Custom Controller written in Go:

```
package main

import (
    "fmt"
    "time"

    "k8s.io/apimachinery/pkg/apis/meta/v1"
    "k8s.io/client-go/kubernetes"
    "k8s.io/client-go/rest"
    "k8s.io/client-go/tools/cache"
    "k8s.io/client-go/util/workqueue"
)

type CustomController struct {
    clientset kubernetes.Interface
    queue     workqueue.RateLimitingInterface
    informer  cache.SharedIndexInformer
}

func main() {
    // Create a Kubernetes clientset using the default configuration
    config, err := rest.InClusterConfig()
    if err != nil {
        panic(err.Error())
    }
    clientset, err := kubernetes.NewForConfig(config)
    if err != nil {
        panic(err.Error())
    }

    // Create a CustomController
    controller := \&CustomController{
        clientset: clientset,
        queue:     workqueue.NewNamedRateLimitingQueue(workqueue.
```

```
            DefaultControllerRateLimiter(), "CustomController"),
        informer: createInformer(clientset),
    }

    // Start the informer and the worker
    stop := make(chan struct{})
    defer close(stop)
    go controller.informer.Run(stop)
    go controller.runWorker(stop)

    // Wait forever
    select {}
}
```

Chapter 5

Expert

5.1 Describe the Kubernetes scheduler's algorithm for placing Pods on Nodes, considering factors like resource requirements, affinity rules, and taints/-tolerations.

The Kubernetes scheduler is responsible for placing Pods onto Nodes in a cluster based on various constraints and requirements. When a Pod is created, the scheduler evaluates the Pod's specifications, including its resource requirements, affinity rules, and taints/tolerations, to determine the best Node to place the Pod on.

Here are the steps involved in the Kubernetes scheduler algorithm:

Filter Nodes: The scheduler starts by filtering out Nodes that cannot accommodate the Pod's resource requirements. It does this by comparing the resource requests of the Pod with the available resources on each Node.

For example, if a Pod requires 1GB of memory and 2 CPUs, the scheduler will eliminate Nodes with less than 1GB of available memory or 2 CPUs. This filtering process ensures that only Nodes with sufficient resources are considered for scheduling the Pod.

Rank Nodes: Once the scheduler has filtered out Nodes that cannot accommodate the Pod's resource requirements, it assigns a score to each remaining Node based on a set of rules. The Node with the highest score is chosen as the best fit for the Pod.

The score is calculated based on various factors, including the Pod's affinity rules, taints/tolerations, and other scheduling constraints. For example, if a Pod has an affinity rule to run on Nodes with a certain label, the scheduler will give a higher score to Nodes that have that label.

Bind Pod to Node: After ranking the Nodes, the scheduler binds the Pod to the Node with the highest score. If the chosen Node becomes unavailable, the scheduler will select the next best Node and attempt to bind the Pod to that Node.

Here are some examples to illustrate how the Kubernetes scheduler algorithm works:

Example 1: Resource Requirements Suppose we have a cluster with three Nodes, and a Pod with the following resource requirements:

CPU: 2

Memory: 4GB

If Node 1 has 2 CPUs and 8GB of memory, Node 2 has 4 CPUs and 4GB of memory, and Node 3 has 2 CPUs and 2GB of memory, the scheduler will eliminate Node 3 since it does not have enough memory to accommodate the Pod.

The scheduler will then assign a score to Node 1 and Node 2 based on the Pod's resource requirements. Since Node 2 has more CPUs than Node 1, it will have a higher score. Therefore, the scheduler will place the Pod on Node 2.

Example 2: Affinity Rules

Suppose we have a cluster with three Nodes, and a Pod with an affinity rule to run on Nodes with the label "zone=west". If Node 1 has the label "zone=east", Node 2 has the label "zone=west", and Node 3 has no label, the scheduler will assign a higher score to Node 2 because it satisfies the Pod's affinity rule. Therefore, the scheduler will place the Pod on Node 2.

Example 3: Taints and Tolerations

Suppose we have a cluster with three Nodes, and a Pod with a toleration for the taint "dedicated=special". If Node 1 has the taint "dedicated=highmem", Node 2 has the taint "dedicated=highcpu", and Node 3 has no taints, the scheduler will eliminate Node 1 and Node 2 since they have taints that the Pod cannot tolerate.

The scheduler will then assign a score to Node 3 based on other constraints, such as resource requirements and affinity rules. Since Node 3 is the only remaining

5.2   Explain the role of etcd in Kubernetes and its importance in maintaining the cluster's state.

etcd is a distributed key-value store that serves as the primary datastore for Kubernetes. It stores all the configuration data and the state information of the Kubernetes cluster. etcd is a crucial component of Kubernetes, as it ensures the consistency and availability of the cluster's state.

Here are some key features and benefits of etcd in Kubernetes:

Distributed key-value store: etcd is a distributed key-value store that can be accessed by multiple nodes simultaneously. It is designed to be highly available and fault-tolerant, ensuring that the cluster's state is always accessible.

Consistency and coordination: etcd uses a consensus algorithm to ensure that all nodes in the cluster have a consistent view of the cluster's state. It also provides a coordination mechanism to prevent conflicts when multiple nodes attempt to modify the same data simultaneously.

Configuration data storage: etcd stores all the configuration data

for the Kubernetes cluster, including information about Nodes,
Pods, Services, Deployments, and other objects. This data is stored
in a hierarchical key-value format, making it easy to access and manipulate.

State information storage: etcd also stores the state information
for the Kubernetes cluster, such as the current status of Pods and
Nodes, the allocation of resources, and other runtime data. This
information is used by various Kubernetes components, such as
the API server and the scheduler, to make decisions about the
scheduling and deployment of workloads.

API server integration: etcd is integrated with the Kubernetes
API server, which allows Kubernetes administrators and developers to interact with etcd using the Kubernetes API. This integration makes it easy to manage and monitor the cluster's state using
familiar Kubernetes tools and interfaces.

Here's an example to illustrate the importance of etcd in Kubernetes:

Suppose we have a Kubernetes cluster with three Nodes. When a
new Pod is created, the Kubernetes API server updates the Pod's
configuration data in etcd. The scheduler then reads the configuration data from etcd to determine which Node to schedule the
Pod on.

Once the Pod is scheduled, the Kubernetes API server updates the
state information for the Pod in etcd. This includes information
about the Pod's status, resource usage, and other runtime data.
Other Kubernetes components, such as the kubelet and the container runtime, also update the state information in etcd as they
manage the Pod's lifecycle.

If etcd were to fail or become unavailable, the Kubernetes cluster
would be unable to maintain its state. This could lead to incon-
sistencies between the configuration data and the runtime state,
causing Pods to fail or become unavailable. Therefore, the availability and reliability of etcd are critical for the smooth operation
of a Kubernetes cluster.

5.3 How do you configure and manage Role-Based Access Control (RBAC) for cluster resources in Kubernetes?

Role-Based Access Control (RBAC) is a mechanism in Kubernetes that controls access to cluster resources based on the roles and permissions assigned to users and service accounts. RBAC allows Kubernetes administrators to define fine-grained access control policies that restrict access to sensitive resources and operations.

Here are the steps involved in configuring and managing RBAC in Kubernetes:

Define Roles and RoleBindings: The first step in configuring RBAC is to define Roles and RoleBindings. A Role defines a set of permissions for a specific namespace, while a RoleBinding associates a Role with a user or service account.

For example, a Role might grant read-only access to Pods and Services in a namespace, while a RoleBinding might associate the Role with a user or service account, such as a developer or a CI/CD pipeline.

Here's an example YAML file for defining a Role that grants read-only access to Pods and Services in the "default" namespace:

```
kind: Role
apiVersion: rbac.authorization.k8s.io/v1
metadata:
  name: pod-reader
  namespace: default
rules:
- apiGroups: [""] \# "" indicates the core API group
  resources: ["pods", "services"]
  verbs: ["get", "watch", "list"]
```

Here's an example YAML file for defining a RoleBinding that associates the Role with a user or service account:

```
kind: RoleBinding
apiVersion: rbac.authorization.k8s.io/v1
metadata:
  name: read-pods-services
  namespace: default
subjects:
- kind: User
  name: john@example.com
roleRef:
```

```
kind: Role
name: pod-reader
apiGroup: rbac.authorization.k8s.io
```

Apply Roles and RoleBindings: Once Roles and RoleBindings have been defined, they need to be applied to the Kubernetes cluster using the kubectl apply command.

For example, to apply the Role and RoleBinding YAML files defined above, you can use the following commands:

```
kubectl apply -f role.yaml
kubectl apply -f rolebinding.yaml
```

Verify Access: After applying the Roles and RoleBindings, you can verify access to cluster resources using the kubectl auth can-i command.

For example, to verify if a user john@example.com has read access to Pods and Services in the "default" namespace, you can use the following command:

```
kubectl auth can-i get pods,services --namespace=default --as=
    john@example.com
```

This command will return either "yes" or "no" depending on whether the user has the required permissions.

Here are some additional best practices for configuring and managing RBAC in Kubernetes:

Follow the principle of least privilege when defining Roles and RoleBindings. Only grant the minimum level of permissions required for a user or service account to perform their tasks. Regularly audit and review RBAC policies to ensure they are up-to-date and aligned with the organization's security policies. Use service accounts for applications and workloads that require access to cluster resources. Service accounts can be assigned Roles and RoleBindings, just like users, but have the advantage of being managed and rotated automatically by Kubernetes.

5.4 Discuss the process of setting up and managing multi-tenant Kubernetes clusters, including resource quotas and Namespace isolation.

A multi-tenant Kubernetes cluster is a shared environment where multiple teams or applications can run their workloads on the same infrastructure. To ensure that each tenant is isolated and has the resources they need, Kubernetes provides several mechanisms for resource management and Namespace isolation.

Here are the steps involved in setting up and managing multi-tenant Kubernetes clusters:

Create Namespaces: The first step in setting up a multi-tenant Kubernetes cluster is to create Namespaces for each tenant. A Namespace is a virtual cluster that provides a way to partition a single Kubernetes cluster into multiple virtual clusters.

For example, you can create a Namespace called "finance" for the finance team, and a Namespace called "marketing" for the marketing team. Each Namespace will have its own set of resources, such as Pods, Services, and ConfigMaps, and can be managed independently.

Here's an example command for creating a Namespace in Kubernetes:

```
kubectl create namespace finance
```

Set Resource Quotas: Once Namespaces are created, you can set resource quotas to limit the amount of CPU, memory, and storage resources that each tenant can consume. Resource quotas ensure that tenants do not exceed their allocated resources and impact the performance of other tenants in the cluster.

For example, you can set a resource quota for the finance team's Namespace to limit their CPU usage to 2 cores and memory usage to 4GB, like this:

```
apiVersion: v1
kind: ResourceQuota
metadata:
```

```
  name: finance-quota
  namespace: finance
spec:
  hard:
    cpu: "2"
    memory: 4Gi
```

Define Network Policies: To ensure isolation between Namespaces, you can define network policies that restrict network traffic between Namespaces. Network policies can be used to specify which Pods can communicate with each other based on their labels and namespaces.

For example, you can define a network policy that allows traffic between Pods in the same Namespace but blocks traffic between Pods in different Namespaces, like this:

```
apiVersion: networking.k8s.io/v1
kind: NetworkPolicy
metadata:
  name: allow-same-namespace
  namespace: finance
spec:
  podSelector: {}
  policyTypes:
  - Ingress
  ingress:
  - from:
    - podSelector: {}
```

Monitor and Manage Usage: Once the multi-tenant Kubernetes cluster is set up, it's important to monitor resource usage and manage quotas to ensure that tenants do not exceed their allocated resources. Kubernetes provides various tools for monitoring resource usage, such as the Kubernetes Dashboard and the Prometheus monitoring system.

For example, you can use the Kubernetes Dashboard to view resource usage for each Namespace, and adjust resource quotas if necessary.

In summary, setting up and managing a multi-tenant Kubernetes cluster involves creating Namespaces for each tenant, setting resource quotas to limit resource usage, defining network policies to ensure isolation, and monitoring and managing resource usage to ensure optimal performance.

5.5 Explain how Kubernetes handles container networking using different CNI plugins and their pros and cons.

Kubernetes uses a pluggable architecture for container networking, allowing administrators to choose from a variety of Container Network Interface (CNI) plugins to implement networking between Pods and Nodes. CNI plugins are responsible for configuring the network interfaces of Pods and Nodes, and for providing network connectivity between them.

Here are some of the most popular CNI plugins used in Kubernetes, along with their pros and cons:

Flannel: Flannel is a simple and lightweight CNI plugin that uses a virtual overlay network to provide connectivity between Pods and Nodes. Flannel is popular in Kubernetes clusters because it is easy to install and configure, and can be used in a variety of network topologies.

Pros:

Easy to install and configure

Supports a variety of network topologies

Lightweight and low overhead

Cons:

Limited feature set compared to other CNI plugins

Requires a separate configuration store (etcd) for storing network information

Calico: Calico is a powerful and flexible CNI plugin that provides advanced network features such as network policies, security controls, and service mesh integration. Calico uses a combination of BGP and iptables to provide network connectivity between Pods and Nodes.

Pros:

Advanced network features such as network policies and security controls

Scalable and resilient

Integrates well with service meshes

Cons:

More complex to install and configure compared to other CNI plugins

Requires a lot of resources and overhead to operate at scale

Weave Net: Weave Net is a CNI plugin that uses a virtual overlay network to provide network connectivity between Pods and Nodes. Weave Net is designed to be simple and easy to use, making it a popular choice for small and medium-sized Kubernetes clusters.

Pros:

Easy to install and configure

Lightweight and low overhead

Supports a variety of network topologies

Cons:

Limited feature set compared to other CNI plugins

May not scale well for larger clusters

Cilium: Cilium is a CNI plugin that uses eBPF (extended Berkeley Packet Filter) to provide advanced network features such as network policies, security controls, and service mesh integration. Cilium is designed to be highly scalable and resilient, making it a popular choice for large-scale Kubernetes deployments.

Pros:

Advanced network features such as network policies and security controls

Scalable and resilient

Integrates well with service meshes

Cons:

More complex to install and configure compared to other CNI plugins

Requires a lot of resources and overhead to operate at scale

Overall, the choice of CNI plugin depends on the specific requirements of the Kubernetes deployment. Smaller clusters may benefit from lightweight and easy-to-use plugins such as Flannel or Weave Net, while larger and more complex deployments may require more advanced features such as network policies and security controls provided by Calico or Cilium.

5.6 Describe the process of migrating applications between Kubernetes clusters, including strategies for data migration and zero-downtime deployments.

Migrating applications between Kubernetes clusters can be a complex and challenging task, especially when dealing with stateful applications that require data migration. Here are the general steps involved in migrating applications between Kubernetes clusters:

Prepare the new cluster: The first step in migrating applications is to prepare the new Kubernetes cluster. This involves setting up the cluster infrastructure, creating Namespaces, and configuring the necessary resources such as storage classes and network policies.

Deploy the applications: Once the new cluster is ready, the next step is to deploy the applications to the new cluster. This can be done using Kubernetes manifests or other deployment tools such as Helm. It's important to ensure that the applications are compatible with the new cluster's architecture and resources.

Migrate data: If the applications require data migration, this step involves moving the data from the old cluster to the new cluster. There are several strategies for data migration, such as using data synchronization tools like rsync or using data migration tools such as Velero.

Test and validate: Once the applications and data have been migrated, it's important to test and validate the functionality of the applications on the new cluster. This can involve running automated tests, manual testing, and user acceptance testing.

Switch over: Once the applications have been validated, the final step is to switch over the traffic to the new cluster. This can be done using techniques such as DNS switchover or load balancer configuration changes.

Strategies for data migration:

Backup and restore: This involves taking a backup of the data on the old cluster and restoring it on the new cluster. This strategy works well for smaller datasets and stateless applications.

Synchronization: This involves using data synchronization tools such as rsync or object storage sync to transfer data between clusters. This strategy works well for larger datasets and stateful applications.

Strategies for zero-downtime deployments:

Blue/Green deployments: This involves deploying the new version of the application alongside the old version, and gradually shifting traffic to the new version. This strategy works well for stateless applications.

Canary deployments: This involves deploying the new version of the application to a small subset of users, and gradually increasing the percentage of traffic to the new version. This strategy works well for applications with a large user base.

Rolling deployments: This involves deploying the new version of the application to a few Pods at a time, and gradually rolling out the new version to all Pods. This strategy works well for stateful applications.

In summary, migrating applications between Kubernetes clusters involves preparing the new cluster, deploying the applications, migrating data if necessary, testing and validating, and switching over the traffic. Strategies for data migration and zero-downtime deployments should be chosen based on the specific requirements of the applications being migrated.

5.7 Explain how to set up and configure a service mesh like Istio or Linkerd in a Kubernetes environment, and discuss its benefits and challenges.

A service mesh is a layer of infrastructure that provides network and security features for microservices in a Kubernetes environment. Service meshes like Istio or Linkerd can be used to manage traffic between microservices, provide security features such as mTLS (mutual Transport Layer Security), and provide observability and tracing features for microservices.

Here are the general steps involved in setting up and configuring a service mesh in a Kubernetes environment:

Install the service mesh control plane: The first step in setting up a service mesh is to install the control plane, which is the central component that manages the service mesh. This involves installing the Istio or Linkerd control plane using Kubernetes manifests or Helm charts.

Deploy the service mesh sidecars: Once the control plane is installed, the next step is to deploy the service mesh sidecars to the Pods that make up the microservices. This involves modifying the Kubernetes deployment manifests to include the service mesh sidecar containers.

Configure traffic management: Once the service mesh sidecars are deployed, the next step is to configure traffic management rules for the microservices. This can involve setting up traffic routing rules, load balancing, and retries.

Configure security features: Service meshes provide security features such as mTLS for encrypting traffic between microservices. This involves configuring the security policies for the microservices and enabling mTLS for communication between microservices.

Configure observability and tracing: Service meshes provide observability and tracing features for microservices, allowing administrators to monitor and debug the performance of the microservices. This involves configuring the observability and tracing components of the service mesh.

Benefits of using a service mesh:

Traffic management: Service meshes provide traffic management features that simplify the management of microservices traffic, such as traffic routing, load balancing, and retries.

Security: Service meshes provide security features such as mTLS for encrypting traffic between microservices, and access control for restricting access to microservices.

Observability: Service meshes provide observability and tracing features that allow administrators to monitor and debug the performance of the microservices.

Challenges of using a service mesh:

Complexity: Service meshes add an additional layer of complexity to the Kubernetes environment, which can make it more difficult to manage.

Performance overhead: Service meshes can introduce performance overhead due to the additional network hops and encryption/decryption required for mTLS.

Configuration management: Configuring and managing the service mesh can be challenging, particularly for large-scale deployments with many microservices.

In summary, setting up and configuring a service mesh in a Kubernetes environment involves installing the control plane, deploying the service mesh sidecars, configuring traffic management, security features, and observability and tracing. Service meshes provide benefits such as traffic management, security, and observability, but can also introduce challenges such as complexity, performance overhead, and configuration management.

5.8 How do you monitor and manage the performance of a Kubernetes cluster, including identifying bottlenecks and optimizing resource usage?

Monitoring and managing the performance of a Kubernetes cluster is important to ensure that the cluster is running efficiently and to prevent performance bottlenecks that can impact application performance. Here are some of the key steps involved in monitoring and managing the performance of a Kubernetes cluster:

Monitoring cluster resources: The first step in monitoring a Kubernetes cluster is to monitor the cluster resources, including CPU, memory, and storage usage. This can be done using tools such as Prometheus or the Kubernetes Dashboard.

Monitoring application performance: In addition to monitoring cluster resources, it's important to monitor the performance of the applications running on the cluster. This can involve monitoring application response times, error rates, and throughput.

Identifying bottlenecks: Once the cluster resources and application performance are being monitored, the next step is to identify performance bottlenecks. This can involve analyzing metrics and logs to identify resource constraints, network issues, or application performance issues.

Optimizing resource usage: Once bottlenecks are identified, the next step is to optimize resource usage to improve performance. This can involve adjusting resource requests and limits, scaling up or down the number of replicas, or optimizing network settings.

Scaling the cluster: If resource optimization is not enough to address performance issues, the next step is to scale the cluster by adding more Nodes or increasing the size of existing Nodes.

Here are some specific examples of tools and techniques for monitoring and managing the performance of a Kubernetes cluster:

Prometheus: Prometheus is a popular open-source monitoring tool that can be used to monitor cluster resources and application performance in Kubernetes. Prometheus provides a flexible query language and a powerful alerting system.

Grafana: Grafana is a visualization tool that can be used to display metrics and logs collected by Prometheus. Grafana provides a variety of visualization options and allows for easy customization of dashboards.

Horizontal Pod Autoscaler: The Horizontal Pod Autoscaler (HPA) can be used to automatically scale the number of replicas based on resource usage or application performance metrics. The HPA can be configured to scale up or down the number of replicas as needed.

Kubernetes Event API: The Kubernetes Event API provides a way to monitor events happening in the Kubernetes cluster, such as Pod creation or deletion. This can be useful for troubleshooting issues or identifying potential performance bottlenecks.

In summary, monitoring and managing the performance of a Kubernetes cluster involves monitoring cluster resources and application performance, identifying bottlenecks, optimizing resource usage, and scaling the cluster as needed. Tools and techniques such as Prometheus, Grafana, HPA, and the Kubernetes Event API can be used to help monitor and manage the performance of a Kubernetes cluster.

5.9 Describe the process of integrating Kubernetes with third-party services and tools like CI/CD pipelines, monitoring platforms, and external authentication providers.

Kubernetes is a powerful container orchestration platform, but it can be even more powerful when integrated with third-party services and tools. Here are some of the most common scenarios for integrating Kubernetes:

CI/CD pipelines: Kubernetes can be integrated with popular CI/CD pipelines such as Jenkins, GitLab CI/CD, or CircleCI to automate the deployment of applications to Kubernetes clusters. This involves configuring the pipeline to build and package the application, and then using Kubernetes manifests or Helm charts to deploy the application to the Kubernetes cluster.

Monitoring platforms: Kubernetes can be integrated with monitoring platforms such as Prometheus, Grafana, or Datadog to monitor the performance and health of Kubernetes clusters and applications running on the clusters. This involves configuring the monitoring platform to collect metrics and logs from Kubernetes and the applications running on the cluster, and then using visualization tools to display the data.

External authentication providers: Kubernetes can be integrated with external authentication providers such as LDAP, Active Directory, or OAuth2 to provide centralized authentication and authorization for Kubernetes clusters. This involves configuring Kubernetes to use an authentication provider such as OpenID Connect, and then configuring the provider to authenticate users and grant access to Kubernetes resources.

Here are the general steps involved in integrating Kubernetes with third-party services and tools:

Identify the integration requirements: The first step in integrating Kubernetes with third-party services and tools is to identify the integration requirements. This involves identifying the service or tool to be integrated, and understanding the integration options available.

Configure the integration: Once the integration requirements are identified, the next step is to configure the integration. This involves setting up the necessary configuration files or API keys, and configuring the service or tool to interact with Kubernetes.

Test the integration: Once the integration is configured, it's important to test the integration to ensure that it's working correctly. This involves testing the functionality of the integration, such as deploying an application using a CI/CD pipeline or monitoring the performance of a Kubernetes cluster using a monitoring platform.

Monitor and maintain the integration: Once the integration is in place, it's important to monitor and maintain the integration to ensure that it's working correctly over time. This involves monitoring logs and metrics related to the integration, and updating the integration configuration as needed.

Here are some specific examples of tools and techniques for integrating Kubernetes with third-party services and tools:

Helm: Helm is a popular package manager for Kubernetes that can be used to deploy and manage applications on Kubernetes clusters. Helm provides a way to package Kubernetes manifests and configuration files into a single deployable package, making it easy to deploy applications to Kubernetes clusters.

Kubernetes API: The Kubernetes API provides a way to programmatically interact with Kubernetes clusters, allowing external tools and services to query and manipulate Kubernetes resources. This can be used to integrate Kubernetes with other systems or to automate tasks within Kubernetes.

Kubernetes Webhooks: Kubernetes webhooks provide a way to trigger actions within Kubernetes based on external events, such as a new GitHub commit or a new Docker image push. Webhooks can be used to automate the deployment of applications to Kubernetes clusters or to trigger other Kubernetes-related tasks.

In summary, integrating Kubernetes with third-party services and tools involves identifying the integration requirements, configuring the integration, testing the integration, and monitoring and maintaining the integration over time. Tools and techniques such as Helm, the Kubernetes API, and Kubernetes webhooks can be used to help integrate Kubernetes with third-party services and tools.

5.10   Explain how to implement disaster recovery strategies in a Kubernetes cluster, including backup/restore, multi-cluster replication, and failover.

Disaster recovery strategies are critical for ensuring business continuity in the event of a catastrophic failure in a Kubernetes cluster. There are several strategies that can be implemented to mitigate the impact of such events, including backup and restore, multi-cluster replication, and failover.

Backup and restore: The simplest disaster recovery strategy is to create backups of the Kubernetes cluster and restore them in the event of a failure. Kubernetes supports several backup and restore solutions, including Velero, Kasten, and Stash. These solutions can be used to create periodic backups of the Kubernetes cluster's resources, including the cluster configuration, application manifests, and persistent volumes. In the event of a failure, the backups can be used to restore the cluster to a previous state.

Multi-cluster replication: A more advanced disaster recovery strategy is to use multi-cluster replication to create a replica of the Kubernetes cluster in a separate location. This can be done using tools like Kubernetes Federation, Rancher, or OpenShift. Multi-cluster replication involves replicating the Kubernetes cluster's resources, including the configuration, application manifests, and persistent volumes, to a separate cluster located in a different region or data center. In the event of a failure, the replica cluster can be promoted to the primary cluster, providing a seamless failover experience.

Failover: A more sophisticated disaster recovery strategy is to implement automatic failover in the event of a failure. This involves setting up a secondary Kubernetes cluster that can take over the workload in the event of a failure. This can be done using tools like

Kubernetes StatefulSets or Operators. When a failure is detected, the secondary cluster is automatically promoted to the primary cluster, and traffic is routed to the secondary cluster. Once the primary cluster is restored, traffic can be routed back to the primary cluster.

Here are the general steps involved in implementing disaster recovery strategies in a Kubernetes cluster:

Identify the disaster recovery requirements: The first step in implementing disaster recovery strategies in a Kubernetes cluster is to identify the disaster recovery requirements. This involves identifying the potential failure scenarios and the impact of those failures on the business.

Select the appropriate disaster recovery strategy: Once the disaster recovery requirements are identified, the next step is to select the appropriate disaster recovery strategy. This involves evaluating the benefits and drawbacks of each strategy and selecting the strategy that best meets the requirements.

Implement the disaster recovery strategy: Once the strategy is selected, the next step is to implement the disaster recovery strategy. This involves setting up the necessary infrastructure, configuring the Kubernetes cluster, and testing the failover scenario.

Monitor and maintain the disaster recovery solution: Once the disaster recovery strategy is in place, it's important to monitor and maintain the solution to ensure that it's working correctly over time. This involves monitoring logs and metrics related to the disaster recovery solution, and updating the solution configuration as needed.

Here are some specific examples of tools and techniques for implementing disaster recovery strategies in a Kubernetes cluster:

Velero: Velero is a popular backup and restore solution for Kubernetes clusters. Velero can be used to create backups of the Kubernetes cluster's resources, including the configuration, application manifests, and persistent volumes, and restore them in the event of a failure.

Kubernetes Federation: Kubernetes Federation is a tool that can be used to create a replica of the Kubernetes cluster in a separate location. Kubernetes Federation replicates the Kubernetes cluster's resources, including the configuration, application manifests, and persistent volumes, to a separate cluster located in a different region or data center.

Kubernetes StatefulSets: Kubernetes StatefulSets can be used to implement automatic failover in the event of a failure. StatefulSets ensure that each pod in the cluster has a unique identity and that persistent volumes are attached to the correct pod. This ensures that when a failure occurs

5.11 Discuss the role of the Kubernetes API Aggregation and its use cases in extending the Kubernetes API.

The Kubernetes API Aggregation feature allows custom resources and API servers to be added to a Kubernetes cluster, extending the functionality of the Kubernetes API. This feature allows Kubernetes to be customized to meet the specific needs of an organization or project.

Here are some of the key use cases for Kubernetes API Aggregation:

Custom resources: Kubernetes API Aggregation can be used to create custom resources that are specific to an organization or project. These custom resources can be used to represent complex objects, such as databases or message queues, and can be used in Kubernetes manifests to deploy and manage these objects.

Custom API servers: Kubernetes API Aggregation can be used to create custom API servers that provide additional functionality beyond the standard Kubernetes API. These custom API servers can be used to implement complex workflows, such as approval workflows or custom resource lifecycle management.

Extension points: Kubernetes API Aggregation provides extension points for other Kubernetes components, such as controllers and admission webhooks. This allows these components to interact with the custom resources and API servers that are added to the Kubernetes cluster.

Here's how Kubernetes API Aggregation works:

Custom Resource Definition (CRD): The first step in using Kubernetes API Aggregation is to define a custom resource using the Custom Resource Definition (CRD) API. This involves creating a YAML file that defines the custom resource's schema, validation rules, and default values.

Custom API Server: Once the custom resource is defined, the next step is to create a custom API server that implements the API for the custom resource. This involves creating a Kubernetes Deployment or StatefulSet that runs a custom API server image, which implements the custom resource's API.

Aggregation Layer: The aggregation layer is a Kubernetes API server that aggregates the APIs provided by multiple API servers, including the custom API server. The aggregation layer provides a unified API for the custom resource and other Kubernetes resources.

API Extension: The final step in using Kubernetes API Aggregation is to extend the Kubernetes API to include the custom resource. This involves registering the custom resource with the Kubernetes API server using the aggregation layer's API.

Here are some specific examples of tools and techniques for using Kubernetes API Aggregation:

Kubernetes Operator: Kubernetes Operator is a framework for building and deploying custom controllers that automate the management of complex applications on Kubernetes. Kubernetes Operator can be used in conjunction with Kubernetes API Aggregation to create custom resources and controllers that manage the lifecycle of these resources.

API Server Builder: API Server Builder is a tool that can be used to generate a custom API server image for a custom resource. API Server Builder automates the creation of the Kubernetes Deployment or StatefulSet and the Docker image that runs the custom API server.

In summary, Kubernetes API Aggregation allows custom resources and API servers to be added to a Kubernetes cluster, extending the functionality of the Kubernetes API. Kubernetes API Aggregation can be used to create custom resources, custom API servers, and extension points for other Kubernetes components. Tools and techniques such as Kubernetes Operator and API Server Builder can be used to help implement Kubernetes API Aggregation.

5.12 Describe the process of building custom Kubernetes Operators using tools like Operator SDK and Kubebuilder.

Building custom Kubernetes Operators can be a complex task, but there are tools like Operator SDK and Kubebuilder that simplify the process. Here's a step-by-step guide to building custom Kubernetes Operators using these tools:

Define the custom resource: The first step in building a custom Kubernetes Operator is to define the custom resource that the operator will manage. This involves creating a Custom Resource Definition (CRD) for the resource. The CRD defines the schema and behavior of the custom resource. For example, if you want to build an operator to manage a MySQL database, you would define a CRD that defines the MySQL resource's schema and behavior.

Generate the operator code: Once the custom resource is defined, the next step is to generate the operator code using a tool like Operator SDK or Kubebuilder. Both tools provide templates that generate the scaffolding for the operator code. The generated code includes a controller that manages the lifecycle of the custom resource.

Implement the operator logic: Once the operator code is generated, the next step is to implement the operator logic. This involves writing the code that handles the create, update, and delete operations for the custom resource. For example, if you are building an operator for a MySQL database, you would write the code that creates and manages the MySQL database instances.

Build and deploy the operator: Once the operator code is implemented, the final step is to build and deploy the operator. This involves building a Docker image that includes the operator code and deploying the image to a Kubernetes cluster. The operator can be deployed as a standalone application or as a container within a Kubernetes pod.

Here's how Operator SDK and Kubebuilder simplify the process of building custom Kubernetes Operators:

Operator SDK: Operator SDK is a tool that simplifies the process of building Kubernetes Operators by providing templates and tools that generate the scaffolding for the operator code. The tool provides a choice of programming languages, including Go, Ansible, and Helm, to write the operator code. Operator SDK also includes a suite of tools that automate the build, test, and deployment of the operator.

Kubebuilder: Kubebuilder is a tool that simplifies the process of building Kubernetes Operators by providing a set of libraries and tools that automate the operator development process. Kubebuilder generates the scaffolding for the operator code, including the controller and CRD, and provides libraries that simplify common tasks like logging and error handling. Kubebuilder also includes a set of tools that automate the build, test, and deployment of the operator.

Here are some additional tips for building custom Kubernetes Operators:

Use the Kubernetes API: Kubernetes Operators are built using the Kubernetes API, which provides a powerful set of primitives for managing the lifecycle of Kubernetes resources. Operators can use the Kubernetes API to create, update, and delete resources, as well as to monitor the state of the cluster.

Use controllers: Controllers are a powerful tool for managing the lifecycle of Kubernetes resources. Controllers monitor the state of the cluster and reconcile the desired state with the actual state of the resources. This makes it easy to implement complex workflows, such as multi-step deployment processes and resource cleanup.

Use operator frameworks: Operator SDK and Kubebuilder are examples of operator frameworks that simplify the process of building Kubernetes Operators. These frameworks provide templates, tools, and libraries that automate many of the tasks involved in building an operator. Using an operator framework can save a lot of time and effort in building an operator.

In summary, building custom Kubernetes Operators involves defining the custom resource, generating the operator code, implementing the operator logic, and building and deploying the operator. Tools like Operator SDK and Kubebuilder simplify the process by providing templates, libraries, and tools that automate many of the tasks involved in building an operator

5.13 Explain how to troubleshoot common issues in a Kubernetes environment, including networking, storage, and application-related problems.

Troubleshooting common issues in a Kubernetes environment can be challenging, but there are several approaches that can be used to identify and resolve these issues. Here are some tips and techniques for troubleshooting common issues in a Kubernetes environment:

Networking Issues:

Networking issues are a common problem in Kubernetes environments, and can often be caused by misconfiguration of network policies, services, or pod networking. To troubleshoot networking issues, try the following:

Check the status of Kubernetes networking components, such as kube-proxy and CNI plugins, to ensure that they are running correctly. Check the status of network policies and services to ensure that they are configured correctly and allow traffic to flow between pods and services. Use network diagnostic tools, such as traceroute and tcpdump, to trace the path of network traffic and identify potential bottlenecks or issues. Storage Issues:

Storage issues can arise when pods are unable to access or use persistent volumes or other storage resources. To troubleshoot storage issues, try the following:

Check the status of persistent volumes and persistent volume claims to ensure that they are bound and available for use. Check the status of storage classes to ensure that they are configured correctly and match the requirements of the pod. Use storage diagnostic tools, such as kubectl describe, to view the status and configuration of storage resources. Application-related Issues:

Application-related issues can arise when pods are unable to start or function correctly, due to issues with the pod configuration, environment variables, or application code. To troubleshoot application-related issues, try the following:

Check the logs of the pod and application to identify any error messages or other issues. Use diagnostic tools, such as kubectl exec and kubectl logs, to view the state and output of the application. Check the configuration of the pod and deployment, including environment variables and volume mounts, to ensure that they are configured correctly.

In addition to these specific tips, here are some general best practices for troubleshooting common issues in a Kubernetes environment:

Monitor the Kubernetes environment:

Use monitoring tools, such as Prometheus and Grafana, to monitor the health and performance of the Kubernetes environment. These tools can help identify potential issues before they become critical.

Collect and analyze logs:

Collect and analyze logs from Kubernetes components, pods, and applications using tools like Elasticsearch, Logstash, and Kibana. These tools can help identify patterns and trends that may indicate potential issues.

Use the Kubernetes API:

Use the Kubernetes API to view the state and configuration of

Kubernetes resources, including pods, services, and nodes. The Kubernetes API provides a rich set of diagnostic tools that can be used to troubleshoot issues.

Collaborate with the Kubernetes community:

The Kubernetes community is a rich source of knowledge and expertise. Collaborate with other Kubernetes users and developers in forums like Slack and GitHub to share experiences and learn from others.

In summary, troubleshooting common issues in a Kubernetes environment requires a combination of diagnostic tools, monitoring, and collaboration with the Kubernetes community. By following these best practices and techniques, you can quickly identify and resolve issues in your Kubernetes environment.

5.14 How do you optimize the performance of a Kubernetes cluster in terms of resource usage, scaling, and resiliency?

Optimizing the performance of a Kubernetes cluster is essential for ensuring that applications run smoothly and efficiently. Here are some tips and techniques for optimizing the performance of a Kubernetes cluster:

Resource usage:

Efficient resource usage is critical for optimizing the performance of a Kubernetes cluster. Here are some tips to help optimize resource usage:

Set resource limits: Set resource limits for containers and pods to ensure that they do not consume too many resources. This helps prevent resource contention and improves the overall performance of the cluster.

Use horizontal pod autoscaling: Use horizontal pod autoscaling to automatically scale pods up or down based on resource usage. This helps ensure that resources are efficiently utilized and prevents over-provisioning.

Use resource quotas: Use resource quotas to limit the total amount of resources that can be used by a namespace or user. This helps prevent resource contention and ensures that resources are efficiently utilized. Scaling:

Scaling is critical for ensuring that the Kubernetes cluster can handle the load of running applications. Here are some tips to help optimize scaling:

Use node autoscaling: Use node autoscaling to automatically add or remove nodes based on demand. This helps ensure that the cluster can handle spikes in traffic and prevents over-provisioning.

Use pod autoscaling: Use horizontal pod autoscaling to automatically scale the number of pods based on demand. This helps ensure that the cluster can handle spikes in traffic and prevents over-provisioning.

Resiliency: Ensuring the resiliency of a Kubernetes cluster is essential for ensuring that applications can handle failures and maintain uptime. Here are some tips to help optimize resiliency:

Use high availability: Use high availability configurations for Kubernetes components, such as the API server, etcd, and control plane components. This helps ensure that the cluster can handle failures and maintain uptime.

Use pod anti-affinity: Use pod anti-affinity to ensure that pods are not scheduled on the same node as other pods with similar characteristics. This helps ensure that the cluster can handle failures and maintain uptime.

Use pod disruption budgets: Use pod disruption budgets to ensure that a minimum number of pods are available during node maintenance or failures. This helps ensure that the cluster can handle failures and maintain uptime.

In summary, optimizing the performance of a Kubernetes cluster requires a combination of resource usage, scaling, and resiliency optimizations. By following these best practices and techniques, you can ensure that your Kubernetes cluster runs efficiently and effectively.

5.15 Describe the process of securing a Kubernetes cluster at different levels, including the control plane, worker nodes, and container images.

Securing a Kubernetes cluster is essential to protect it from malicious attacks and ensure the integrity of the applications running on it. Kubernetes provides several built-in security features that can be used to secure the control plane, worker nodes, and container images. Here are some key steps to secure a Kubernetes cluster at different levels:

Securing the Control Plane:

The control plane is the core of the Kubernetes cluster and manages the entire system. To secure the control plane, here are some key steps:

Use TLS encryption: Enable TLS encryption for all Kubernetes API server endpoints to prevent eavesdropping and man-in-the-middle attacks.

Use RBAC: Use Role-Based Access Control (RBAC) to restrict access to Kubernetes resources and ensure that only authorized users and applications can interact with the cluster.

Use secure storage for secrets: Use Kubernetes Secrets to store sensitive data, such as authentication tokens and passwords, and encrypt them at rest to prevent unauthorized access.

Securing Worker Nodes:

Worker nodes run the containerized applications and are critical to the overall security of the cluster. To secure worker nodes, here are some key steps:

Use container runtime security: Use container runtime security features, such as SELinux, AppArmor, or seccomp, to restrict container behavior and prevent malicious attacks.

Use node-level firewalls: Use node-level firewalls, such as iptables or firewalld, to restrict incoming and outgoing traffic to and from the worker nodes.

Use host-based intrusion detection: Use host-based intrusion detection tools, such as Sysdig Falco or OSSEC, to detect and prevent unauthorized access to the worker nodes.

Securing Container Images: Container images are the building blocks of containerized applications and must be secured to prevent malicious attacks. To secure container images, here are some key steps:

Use secure image registries: Use secure image registries, such as Docker Hub or Google Container Registry, to store container images and ensure that they are free from vulnerabilities and malware.

Use container image scanning: Use container image scanning tools, such as Anchore or Clair, to scan container images for vulnerabilities and malware before deploying them to the cluster.

Use image signing and verification: Use image signing and verification tools, such as Notary or Docker Content Trust, to ensure that container images are signed and verified before they are deployed to the cluster.

In summary, securing a Kubernetes cluster requires a multi-layered approach that involves securing the control plane, worker nodes, and container images. By following these best practices and techniques, you can ensure that your Kubernetes cluster is secure and protected from malicious attacks.

5.16 Discuss the role of Kubernetes Federated Clusters and their use cases in multi-region and multi-cloud deployments.

Kubernetes Federated Clusters is a feature that allows you to manage multiple Kubernetes clusters as a single entity. This can be especially useful in multi-region and multi-cloud deployments, where you have clusters running across different geographic locations or cloud providers. Here are some key features and use cases of Kubernetes Federated Clusters:

Centralized management:

With Kubernetes Federated Clusters, you can manage multiple clusters from a single control plane. This allows you to view and manage resources across multiple clusters, and to apply changes to all clusters simultaneously.

Multi-region deployments:

Kubernetes Federated Clusters can be used to manage clusters in different geographic locations. This is useful for applications that need to be deployed close to their users, or for disaster recovery scenarios where you need to have redundant clusters in different regions.

Multi-cloud deployments:

Kubernetes Federated Clusters can be used to manage clusters running on different cloud providers. This is useful for applications that need to be deployed across multiple cloud providers for redundancy or to take advantage of specific cloud features.

Resource sharing:

Kubernetes Federated Clusters allows you to share resources across multiple clusters. This can be useful for applications that require high availability or for applications that need to scale up and down quickly based on demand.

Cross-cluster communication:

Kubernetes Federated Clusters allows you to configure cross-cluster communication between different clusters. This can be useful for applications that need to communicate across different regions or cloud providers.

Some use cases for Kubernetes Federated Clusters include:

Multi-region deployment of applications:

Kubernetes Federated Clusters can be used to manage clusters running in different geographic locations, allowing you to deploy applications closer to their users and to ensure high availability in case of a regional outage.

Multi-cloud deployment of applications:

Kubernetes Federated Clusters can be used to manage clusters running on different cloud providers, allowing you to take advantage of specific cloud features and to ensure high availability in case of a cloud outage.

Resource sharing across clusters:

Kubernetes Federated Clusters can be used to share resources across multiple clusters, allowing you to optimize resource usage and reduce costs.

Cross-cluster communication:

Kubernetes Federated Clusters can be used to configure cross-cluster communication between different clusters, allowing you to build distributed applications that span multiple regions or cloud providers.

In summary, Kubernetes Federated Clusters is a powerful feature that allows you to manage multiple Kubernetes clusters as a single entity. It can be especially useful in multi-region and multi-cloud deployments, where you need to deploy applications across different geographic locations or cloud providers. By using Kubernetes Federated Clusters, you can simplify the management of your Kubernetes environment and ensure high availability and scalability for your applications.

5.17 Explain how to implement end-to-end encryption in a Kubernetes cluster, including securing data at rest and in transit.

Implementing end-to-end encryption in a Kubernetes cluster involves securing data both at rest and in transit. End-to-end encryption ensures that data is encrypted when it is stored and when it is transmitted, providing an extra layer of security to protect sensitive information. Here are some steps to implement end-to-end encryption in a Kubernetes cluster:

Encrypting Data at Rest:

Data at rest refers to data that is stored in a persistent volume or a database. To encrypt data at rest in a Kubernetes cluster, you can use Kubernetes Secrets or external storage solutions like AWS EBS or Google Persistent Disk with encryption enabled.

Using Kubernetes Secrets: Kubernetes Secrets allows you to store sensitive information, such as API keys, passwords, and certificates, as encrypted data in etcd. You can create a Secret object in Kubernetes, which can then be mounted as a volume in a pod to provide secure access to the sensitive data.

Using External Storage Solutions: External storage solutions like AWS EBS and Google Persistent Disk allow you to enable encryption at the storage layer. This ensures that any data written to the storage is encrypted at rest.

Encrypting Data in Transit:

Data in transit refers to data that is transmitted over the network. To encrypt data in transit in a Kubernetes cluster, you can use Transport Layer Security (TLS) or Secure Socket Layer (SSL) certificates.

Using TLS: TLS provides end-to-end encryption for data transmitted over the network. You can enable TLS for the Kubernetes API server, etcd, and other Kubernetes components using a TLS certificate.

Using SSL: SSL certificates provide encryption for data transmitted over the network. You can use SSL certificates for encrypting data transmitted by applications running in pods.

Securing Kubernetes Secrets:

Kubernetes Secrets contain sensitive information and must be secured to prevent unauthorized access. To secure Kubernetes Secrets, you can use Role-Based Access Control (RBAC) to restrict access to Secrets.

Using RBAC: RBAC allows you to restrict access to Kubernetes resources based on user roles and permissions. You can use RBAC to limit access to Secrets only to authorized users and applications.

In summary, implementing end-to-end encryption in a Kubernetes cluster involves securing data both at rest and in transit. You can encrypt data at rest using Kubernetes Secrets or external storage solutions, and encrypt data in transit using TLS or SSL certificates. Additionally, you can use RBAC to secure Kubernetes Secrets and restrict access to sensitive information. By following these best practices, you can ensure that your Kubernetes cluster is secure and protected from unauthorized access.

5.18 Describe the process of setting up and managing autoscaling groups in Kubernetes, including Vertical Pod Autoscaler (VPA) and Cluster Autoscaler.

Autoscaling in Kubernetes refers to the process of dynamically adjusting the number of replicas of a deployment or a replica set based on resource utilization or other metrics. There are two types of autoscaling in Kubernetes: horizontal and vertical autoscaling.

Horizontal Autoscaling:

Horizontal autoscaling involves adding or removing replicas of a deployment or replica set based on resource utilization or other metrics. Kubernetes provides two types of horizontal autoscaling:

Horizontal Pod Autoscaler (HPA): HPA scales the number of replicas of a deployment or replica set based on CPU utilization or custom metrics.

Cluster Autoscaler: Cluster Autoscaler scales the number of nodes in a Kubernetes cluster based on the demand for resources.

Vertical Autoscaling:

Vertical autoscaling involves adjusting the resource allocation of individual pods based on their resource utilization. Kubernetes provides the following types of vertical autoscaling:

Vertical Pod Autoscaler (VPA): VPA adjusts the CPU and memory requests and limits of individual pods based on their resource utilization. This ensures that pods have enough resources to operate efficiently without wasting resources.

Here are the steps to set up and manage autoscaling groups in Kubernetes:

Enable Metrics Server:

To enable autoscaling in Kubernetes, you need to first enable Metrics Server. Metrics Server collects resource utilization data from pods and nodes, which is used by autoscaling controllers to make scaling decisions.

Set Up Horizontal Autoscaling:

To set up horizontal autoscaling in Kubernetes, you need to create a Horizontal Pod Autoscaler (HPA) or a Cluster Autoscaler.

Horizontal Pod Autoscaler: To set up an HPA, you need to define the minimum and maximum number of replicas for a deployment or replica set, and the target CPU utilization or custom metric.

Cluster Autoscaler: To set up Cluster Autoscaler, you need to deploy the Cluster Autoscaler controller and configure it with the minimum and maximum number of nodes for each node group.

Set Up Vertical Autoscaling:

To set up vertical autoscaling in Kubernetes, you need to deploy the Vertical Pod Autoscaler (VPA) controller and configure it to adjust the CPU and memory requests and limits of individual pods based on their resource utilization.

Monitor Autoscaling:

Once autoscaling is enabled, you need to monitor the performance of the autoscaling groups and adjust the scaling thresholds as needed. You can use Kubernetes metrics and logs to monitor the performance of the autoscaling groups and to identify any issues.

In summary, setting up and managing autoscaling groups in Kubernetes involves enabling Metrics Server, setting up horizontal and vertical autoscaling controllers, and monitoring the performance of the autoscaling groups. By following these best practices, you can ensure that your Kubernetes environment is optimized for resource utilization and can handle variable demand for resources.

5.19 How do you ensure data persistence and durability in a Kubernetes cluster, considering factors like node failures, application crashes, and data corruption?

Ensuring data persistence and durability in a Kubernetes cluster is critical to prevent data loss and maintain the availability of applications. Kubernetes provides several mechanisms to ensure data persistence and durability, including persistent volumes, stateful sets, and backup and restore solutions.

Persistent Volumes:

Persistent volumes (PVs) in Kubernetes are used to store data outside of pods, ensuring that the data persists even if the pod is deleted or recreated. PVs can be backed by various storage solutions, such as local storage, network-attached storage (NAS), and cloud storage.

Local Storage: Local storage is a storage solution that uses the local disks on the worker nodes. Local storage provides high performance and low latency, but it is not suitable for data that needs to be shared between pods.

NAS: Network-attached storage (NAS) is a storage solution that provides shared storage over the network. NAS can be used to store data that needs to be shared between pods, such as configuration files and logs.

Cloud Storage: Cloud storage is a storage solution that provides storage on the cloud, such as Amazon EBS or Google Persistent Disk. Cloud storage is highly available and durable, but it may be more expensive than local storage or NAS.

Stateful Sets:

Stateful sets in Kubernetes are used to manage stateful applications, such as databases or message queues. Stateful sets ensure that pods are created and deleted in a specific order, ensuring that the data stored in the pods is preserved even if a pod is deleted or recreated.

Backup and Restore Solutions:

Backup and restore solutions are used to protect data from node failures, application crashes, and data corruption. Backup solutions can be used to create a copy of the data that can be restored in case of a failure, while restore solutions can be used to restore the data from a backup.

Velero: Velero is a backup and restore solution for Kubernetes that can be used to back up and restore persistent volumes, stateful sets, and other Kubernetes resources.

Stash: Stash is a backup and restore solution for Kubernetes that can be used to back up and restore persistent volumes and stateful sets. Stash also provides features like data encryption and compression.

In summary, ensuring data persistence and durability in a Kubernetes cluster involves using persistent volumes to store data outside of pods, using stateful sets to manage stateful applications, and using backup and restore solutions to protect data from node failures, application crashes, and data corruption. By following these best practices, you can ensure that your Kubernetes cluster is resilient and can recover from failures without data loss.

5.20 Discuss the future of Kubernetes and its ecosystem, including potential improvements, emerging technologies, and best practices.

Kubernetes has become the de-facto standard for container orchestration, and its ecosystem is continuously evolving to meet the changing needs of modern application development. Here are some potential improvements, emerging technologies, and best practices that are likely to shape the future of Kubernetes and its ecosystem:

Improvements to Kubernetes Core:

Kubernetes is continuously improving its core components, such as the scheduler, the API server, and the container runtime, to make them more efficient, scalable, and secure. Some potential improvements include:

Improved scalability: Kubernetes is working on improving its scalability by reducing the overhead of the API server and the etcd datastore.

Improved security: Kubernetes is adding new security features, such as network policies and pod security policies, to provide better isolation and control over network traffic and access to resources.

Improved reliability: Kubernetes is adding features such as automated failover and self-healing to improve the reliability of the cluster.

Emerging Technologies:

There are several emerging technologies that are likely to shape the future of Kubernetes and its ecosystem, such as:

Service Mesh: Service mesh technologies like Istio and Linkerd are becoming increasingly popular in Kubernetes environments to manage network traffic and provide advanced security features.

Serverless: Serverless technologies like Knative and OpenFaaS are becoming popular in Kubernetes environments to provide a more lightweight and event-driven approach to application development.

Machine Learning: Kubernetes is increasingly being used as a platform for deploying and managing machine learning workloads, with tools like Kubeflow and TensorFlow.

Best Practices:

As Kubernetes continues to evolve, new best practices are emerging to help organizations get the most out of their Kubernetes deployments. Some of these best practices include:

DevOps Culture: Kubernetes deployments require a strong DevOps culture to ensure that teams are collaborating effectively and can respond quickly to issues.

Multi-Cloud: Kubernetes is increasingly being used to manage multi-cloud environments, allowing organizations to take advantage of the strengths of different cloud providers.

Hybrid Cloud: Kubernetes is also being used to manage hybrid cloud environments, allowing organizations to run applications both on-premises and in the cloud.

In summary, the future of Kubernetes and its ecosystem is promising, with ongoing improvements to the core components, emerging technologies like service mesh and serverless, and new best practices for deployment and management. Organizations that are adopting Kubernetes should stay up-to-date with these trends to ensure that they are taking advantage of the latest features and capabilities.

Chapter 6

Guru

6.1 Explain in detail how the Kubernetes scheduler works, considering factors like scoring, filtering, and prioritization of nodes for Pod placement.

The Kubernetes scheduler is responsible for placing pods onto nodes in the cluster based on available resources, node capacity, and other constraints. The scheduler is a pluggable component in Kubernetes, which means that it can be customized to use different scheduling algorithms based on the requirements of the cluster.

Here is an overview of how the Kubernetes scheduler works:

Scoring:

The scheduler assigns a score to each node in the cluster based on various factors, such as available resources, node affinity, and taints/tolerations. The score is calculated based on a set of heuristics that take into account the constraints and requirements of the pod.

For example, if a pod requires a certain amount of CPU and memory, the scheduler will assign a higher score to nodes that have sufficient resources available to accommodate the pod. If the pod has affinity rules, such as requiring to run on nodes with specific labels or annotations, the scheduler will also assign a higher score to nodes that match the affinity rules.

Filtering:

After assigning scores to each node, the scheduler filters out nodes that do not meet the requirements of the pod. For example, if a pod requires a certain version of an operating system, the scheduler will filter out nodes that do not have the required version installed.

Prioritization:

If multiple nodes meet the requirements of the pod, the scheduler uses prioritization to select the best node. The prioritization algorithm takes into account factors such as resource utilization, node health, and pod priority.

For example, if a node has high resource utilization or is experiencing issues, the scheduler may choose to place the pod on a different node to avoid overloading the node. If the pod has a higher priority, such as being critical to the operation of the cluster, the scheduler will prioritize placing the pod on a node that meets its requirements.

Once the scheduler has selected a node for the pod, it updates the Kubernetes API server with the assignment, and the Kubernetes controller manager takes over to ensure that the pod is deployed and running on the selected node.

In summary, the Kubernetes scheduler is responsible for placing pods onto nodes in the cluster based on available resources, node capacity, and other constraints. The scheduler uses a combination of scoring, filtering, and prioritization to select the best node for the pod, taking into account the requirements and constraints of the pod and the cluster. The scheduler is a pluggable component in Kubernetes, allowing for customization of scheduling algorithms based on the specific requirements of the cluster.

6.2 Discuss the concept of Kubernetes Federation, its architecture, and use cases, including multi-cluster management and cross-cluster service discovery.

Kubernetes Federation is a feature that allows you to manage multiple Kubernetes clusters as a single entity, providing a unified management experience across clusters. Federation provides a number of benefits, including the ability to manage large-scale deployments across multiple clusters, improve fault tolerance and resilience, and simplify cross-cluster service discovery and networking.

Here is an overview of the architecture of Kubernetes Federation and its key components:

Federated Control Plane:

The Federated Control Plane is the central component of Kubernetes Federation, responsible for managing multiple Kubernetes clusters as a single entity. The Federated Control Plane consists of a set of federated API servers, which expose a unified API that can be used to manage resources across multiple clusters.

Federated Resources:

Federated Resources are a set of Kubernetes resources that can be federated across multiple clusters, such as Deployments, Services, ConfigMaps, and Secrets. Federated Resources are defined using a Federated Resource Definition (FRD), which describes the desired state of the resource and how it should be replicated across clusters.

Federated Placement Control:

Federated Placement Control is responsible for determining where federated resources should be placed across multiple clusters. Federated Placement Control takes into account factors such as resource availability, location, and affinity to ensure that resources are placed in the most appropriate clusters.

Federated DNS:

Federated DNS is responsible for providing a unified DNS service across multiple clusters. Federated DNS allows you to easily discover and access services across multiple clusters using a single DNS name.

Now, let's discuss some of the use cases for Kubernetes Federation:

Multi-Cluster Management:

Kubernetes Federation allows you to manage multiple clusters as a single entity, simplifying operations and reducing management overhead. This is particularly useful in large-scale deployments where you need to manage multiple clusters distributed across different regions or cloud providers.

Cross-Cluster Service Discovery:

Kubernetes Federation provides a unified DNS service across multiple clusters, allowing you to easily discover and access services across clusters using a single DNS name. This is particularly useful in microservices architectures, where services are distributed across multiple clusters.

High Availability and Resilience:

Kubernetes Federation provides a way to replicate resources across multiple clusters, improving fault tolerance and resilience. This is particularly useful in mission-critical applications, where downtime can have significant financial or reputational impact.

Disaster Recovery:

Kubernetes Federation provides a way to easily replicate resources across multiple clusters, making it easier to recover from disasters or outages. By replicating resources across multiple clusters, you can ensure that your applications remain available even if one or more clusters go offline.

In summary, Kubernetes Federation allows you to manage multiple Kubernetes clusters as a single entity, providing a unified management experience across clusters. Kubernetes Federation provides a number of benefits, including the ability to manage large-scale deployments across multiple clusters, improve fault tolerance and resilience, and simplify cross-cluster service discovery and networking.

6.3 Describe strategies for backing up and restoring a Kubernetes cluster, including etcd snapshots, Persistent Volume (PV) backups, and restoring API objects.

Backing up and restoring a Kubernetes cluster is essential for ensuring business continuity and recovering from disasters or outages. There are different strategies and tools available for backing up and restoring a Kubernetes cluster, including etcd snapshots, Persistent Volume (PV) backups, and restoring API objects.

Here is an overview of each strategy:

etcd Snapshots:

etcd is the primary data store for Kubernetes, storing all cluster configuration data and state information. Taking regular snapshots of the etcd database is a critical step in backing up a Kubernetes cluster. etcd snapshots can be taken using the etcdctl command-line tool or automated using Kubernetes operators like the etcd backup operator.

For example, to take a snapshot of the etcd database, you can use the following command:

```
\$ etcdctl snapshot save /path/to/snapshot.db
```

To restore the etcd database from a snapshot, you can use the following command:

```
\$ etcdctl snapshot restore /path/to/snapshot.db
```

Persistent Volume Backups:

In addition to etcd backups, you may also need to back up data stored in Persistent Volumes (PVs) used by your applications. PV backups can be performed using tools like Velero, which allows you to take snapshots of PVs and restore them in the same or a different cluster.

For example, to backup a PV using Velero, you can use the following command:

```
\$ velero backup create my-backup --include-namespaces my-namespace
    --include-resources persistentvolumes
```

To restore a PV backup using Velero, you can use the following command:

```
\$ velero restore create --from-backup my-backup
```

Restoring API Objects:

In addition to backing up data stored in etcd and PVs, you may also need to restore Kubernetes API objects like Deployments, Services, and ConfigMaps. API object backups can be performed using tools like Velero, which allows you to take snapshots of API objects and restore them in the same or a different cluster.

For example, to backup API objects using Velero, you can use the following command:

```
\$ velero backup create my-backup --include-namespaces my-namespace
    --include-resources deployments,services,configmaps
```

To restore API object backups using Velero, you can use the following command:

```
\$ velero restore create --from-backup my-backup
```

In summary, backing up and restoring a Kubernetes cluster is essential for ensuring business continuity and recovering from disasters or outages. Strategies for backing up and restoring a Kubernetes cluster include etcd snapshots, Persistent Volume (PV) backups, and restoring API objects. Tools like Velero can be used to automate and simplify the backup and restore process.

6.4   How do you implement advanced security measures in a Kubernetes cluster, such as encryption at rest, mutual TLS authentication, and image signing?

Implementing advanced security measures in a Kubernetes cluster is critical to protecting sensitive data and preventing unauthorized access. Here are some key strategies and tools for implementing advanced security measures in a Kubernetes cluster:

Encryption at Rest:

Encryption at rest is the process of encrypting data stored in persistent storage like disks and volumes. Kubernetes supports encryption at rest using volume plugins like dm-crypt, which encrypts data on the node before it's written to disk.

To implement encryption at rest in Kubernetes, you need to configure the storage provider to use encryption. For example, in AWS, you can enable encryption for EBS volumes using the AWS Encryption SDK.

Mutual TLS Authentication:

Mutual TLS authentication is a security technique that uses SSL/TLS certificates to authenticate both the server and the client. In Kubernetes, mutual TLS authentication can be implemented using the Kubernetes certificate authority (CA) and service accounts.

To implement mutual TLS authentication in Kubernetes, you need to generate and distribute certificates to clients and servers. Kubernetes provides a built-in CA that can be used to generate and sign certificates for both client and server authentication.

Image Signing:

Image signing is the process of verifying the authenticity and integrity of container images. Kubernetes supports image signing using Notary, a tool for signing and verifying container images.

To implement image signing in Kubernetes, you need to configure Notary to sign and verify images. Notary uses a combination of cryptographic keys and digital signatures to sign and verify images, ensuring that they are authentic and have not been tampered with.

Network Policies:

Network policies are a Kubernetes feature that enables you to control network traffic between pods and services. Network policies can be used to implement advanced security measures like whitelisting or blacklisting traffic based on the source IP address or the port number.

To implement network policies in Kubernetes, you need to define and apply network policies to the appropriate pods and services. Kubernetes provides a declarative way to define network policies using YAML files.

Secrets Management:

Secrets management is the process of securely storing and managing sensitive data like passwords, tokens, and keys. Kubernetes provides a built-in secrets management feature that enables you to store and manage secrets as Kubernetes objects.

To implement secrets management in Kubernetes, you need to create and manage secrets using the Kubernetes API. Secrets can be stored as plain text or as base64-encoded data and can be mounted as files or environment variables in pods.

In summary, implementing advanced security measures in a Kubernetes cluster is critical to protecting sensitive data and preventing unauthorized access. Strategies for implementing advanced security measures in Kubernetes include encryption at rest, mutual TLS authentication, image signing, network policies, and secrets management. Tools like Notary and the Kubernetes API can be used to implement these security measures in a Kubernetes cluster.

6.5 Explain the process of developing and deploying custom Kubernetes controllers, including their design patterns, lifecycle management, and integration with the cluster.

Developing and deploying custom Kubernetes controllers is a key aspect of extending and customizing the functionality of Kubernetes. In this answer, we will discuss the process of developing and deploying custom Kubernetes controllers, including their design patterns, lifecycle management, and integration with the cluster.

Design patterns:

Custom Kubernetes controllers can be developed using several design patterns, including the Informer/Workqueue pattern, the Control Loop pattern, and the Operator pattern. Each of these patterns has its own strengths and weaknesses and can be used to develop controllers for different use cases.

The Informer/Workqueue pattern is a common design pattern used in Kubernetes controllers. This pattern uses a Kubernetes Informer to watch for changes to resources and a Workqueue to manage the processing of those changes. The Informer/Workqueue pattern is useful for controllers that need to react quickly to changes in resources.

The Control Loop pattern is another common design pattern used in Kubernetes controllers. This pattern uses a loop to watch for changes to resources and take action when changes are detected. The Control Loop pattern is useful for controllers that need to take more complex actions based on changes in resources.

The Operator pattern is a more advanced design pattern that combines the Informer/Workqueue pattern and the Control Loop pattern. This pattern is useful for controllers that need to manage the entire lifecycle of a Kubernetes application.

Lifecycle management:

The lifecycle of a custom Kubernetes controller can be managed using tools like Operator SDK and Kubebuilder. These tools provide a framework for developing, deploying, and managing Kubernetes controllers.

The Operator SDK is a set of tools that enables developers to build Kubernetes controllers using the Operator pattern. The SDK includes templates, code generators, and a testing framework for building and testing operators.

Kubebuilder is another tool that can be used to build Kubernetes controllers. Kubebuilder provides a set of libraries and tools for building controllers using the Informer/Workqueue pattern and the Control Loop pattern.

Integration with the cluster:

Custom Kubernetes controllers can be integrated with the cluster using Kubernetes APIs and custom resources. Kubernetes APIs can be used to manage the lifecycle of the controller, while custom resources can be used to define the behavior of the controller.

For example, a custom resource definition (CRD) can be used to define a new resource type, such as a database or a message queue. The custom controller can then use the Kubernetes API to manage the lifecycle of the new resource type.

In summary, developing and deploying custom Kubernetes controllers involves choosing a design pattern, managing the controller's lifecycle, and integrating the controller with the cluster using Kubernetes APIs and custom resources. Tools like Operator SDK and Kubebuilder can be used to simplify the process of developing and deploying custom Kubernetes controllers.

6.6 Discuss the role of service meshes in complex Kubernetes environments, including traffic management, security, and observability features, and compare different service mesh solutions.

In a complex Kubernetes environment, a service mesh can play a critical role in managing and securing the communication between microservices. A service mesh is essentially a dedicated infrastructure layer for managing service-to-service communication, and it typically provides features like traffic management, security, and observability.

Traffic Management: A service mesh can help manage the routing and load balancing of traffic between microservices. By using a service mesh, developers can implement complex routing rules, like canary deployments, blue-green deployments, and A/B testing.

Examples of popular service meshes that offer advanced traffic management features are Istio and Linkerd.

Security: A service mesh can provide advanced security features like mutual TLS authentication, encryption, and authorization. By encrypting all traffic between services, a service mesh can help prevent data breaches and man-in-the-middle attacks.

Istio, for example, provides a robust security framework that enables secure communication between microservices. It includes features like mutual TLS authentication, encryption, and fine-grained access control policies.

Observability: A service mesh can also provide observability features like tracing, monitoring, and logging. By providing insights into the performance and behavior of microservices, a service mesh can help developers diagnose and fix issues more quickly.

Popular service meshes like Istio and Linkerd offer observability features like distributed tracing and metrics collection. They integrate with popular monitoring tools like Prometheus and Grafana to provide real-time insights into the health of the microservices.

Service Mesh Solutions: There are several service mesh solutions available, with different strengths and weaknesses.

Istio is a popular service mesh solution that is widely used in production environments. It provides advanced features like traffic management, security, and observability, and integrates well with Kubernetes.

Linkerd is another service mesh solution that is known for its simplicity and ease of use. It provides advanced features like traffic management, security, and observability, but is considered more lightweight than Istio.

Consul is another service mesh solution that provides advanced features like service discovery, health checking, and service segmentation. It also has a robust API and can be used to manage services in multi-cloud environments.

In summary, service meshes can provide critical features like traffic management, security, and observability in complex Kubernetes environments. Popular service mesh solutions like Istio, Linkerd, and Consul offer different strengths and weaknesses, and the choice of service mesh solution depends on the specific needs of the organization.

6.7 Describe strategies for optimizing the performance of a Kubernetes cluster, including cluster autoscaling, optimizing resource usage, and implementing advanced Pod placement.

Optimizing the performance of a Kubernetes cluster can involve several strategies that aim to improve its scalability, resource utilization, and resiliency. Here are some of the key strategies:

Cluster Autoscaling: One of the most effective ways to optimize the performance of a Kubernetes cluster is to implement cluster autoscaling. This allows the cluster to dynamically scale up or down based on the workload demand, thereby ensuring optimal resource utilization and cost-efficiency.

Cluster autoscaling can be implemented using tools like Kubernetes Cluster Autoscaler (CA) or Horizontal Pod Autoscaler (HPA), which automatically adjust the number of nodes or Pods in the cluster based on the metrics like CPU usage or memory consumption.

Optimizing Resource Usage: Optimizing the resource usage of a Kubernetes cluster can help maximize its performance and reduce costs. This can involve several strategies, including: Right-sizing: Ensuring that each Pod and node is allocated the appropriate amount of resources can help prevent resource wastage and improve performance. Resource limits: Setting resource limits for Pods can help prevent resource contention and improve the stability of the cluster. Resource requests: Specifying resource requests for Pods can help the Kubernetes scheduler make better decisions about Pod placement and improve the overall performance of the cluster. Advanced Pod Placement: The Kubernetes scheduler has advanced features like affinity and anti-affinity rules, node selectors, and tolerations that can be used to optimize Pod placement and improve the performance of the cluster.

For example, using node affinity rules, Pods can be scheduled on specific nodes based on their labels or node attributes. This can help ensure that Pods are placed on nodes that have the required resources, reducing the chances of resource contention.

Using Caching and CDN: Caching and Content Delivery Networks (CDNs) can be used to optimize the performance of Kubernetes applications by reducing the load on the cluster. Caching can be used to store frequently accessed data, while CDNs can be used to distribute content to users from nearby locations, reducing latency and improving the overall user experience.

In summary, optimizing the performance of a Kubernetes cluster involves several strategies, including cluster autoscaling, optimizing resource usage, implementing advanced Pod placement, and using caching and CDNs. By implementing these strategies, organizations can ensure that their Kubernetes applications are scalable, resilient, and performant.

6.8 How do you manage and monitor large-scale, multi-cluster Kubernetes environments, including centralized logging, observability, and alerting?

Managing and monitoring large-scale, multi-cluster Kubernetes environments can be challenging due to the complexity and scale of the deployment. However, there are several tools and best practices that can help organizations effectively manage and monitor their Kubernetes environments. Here are some of the key strategies:

Centralized Logging: Centralized logging is essential for monitoring Kubernetes clusters and identifying issues quickly. Popular logging solutions include Elasticsearch, Fluentd, and Kibana (EFK), which allow organizations to aggregate and analyze logs from multiple clusters.

Observability: Observability is crucial for monitoring and troubleshooting large-scale Kubernetes deployments. It involves collecting and analyzing metrics, traces, and logs to gain insights into the behavior of the system. Tools like Prometheus, Grafana, and Jaeger can be used for observability, providing real-time monitoring, visualization, and alerting capabilities.

Alerting: Effective alerting is critical for identifying and responding to issues in a timely manner. Kubernetes provides a native alerting system through the Kubernetes Event API, which can be used to trigger alerts when certain events occur. Additionally, tools like Prometheus Alertmanager and Grafana Alerting can be used to configure and manage alerts.

Multi-Cluster Management: Managing large-scale, multi-cluster Kubernetes environments can be challenging, especially when dealing with multiple clusters across different regions and clouds. Tools like Kubernetes Federation and Rancher can be used for multi-cluster management, providing a centralized interface for managing and monitoring multiple clusters.

Automation: Automation is essential for managing and monitoring large-scale Kubernetes environments efficiently. Tools like Ansible,

Puppet, and Terraform can be used for automating the deployment and management of Kubernetes clusters, ensuring consistency and reducing the risk of errors.

In summary, managing and monitoring large-scale, multi-cluster Kubernetes environments requires a combination of centralized logging, observability, alerting, multi-cluster management, and automation. By implementing these strategies, organizations can effectively manage and monitor their Kubernetes environments, ensuring optimal performance, scalability, and reliability.

6.9 Discuss the challenges and best practices in implementing multi-cloud and hybrid cloud Kubernetes deployments, including networking, storage, and resource management.

Implementing multi-cloud and hybrid cloud Kubernetes deployments can be challenging due to the complexity of managing resources across different cloud providers and on-premise data centers. Here are some of the key challenges and best practices for addressing them:

Networking: One of the biggest challenges in multi-cloud and hybrid cloud Kubernetes deployments is networking. Since different cloud providers and on-premise data centers have their own networking models, it can be difficult to ensure seamless connectivity between nodes and services. One solution to this challenge is to use a service mesh like Istio or Linkerd, which provide a consistent networking layer across multiple clouds and on-premise environments.

Storage: Another challenge in multi-cloud and hybrid cloud Kubernetes deployments is storage. Different cloud providers and on-premise data centers have their own storage solutions and APIs, which can make it challenging to manage and migrate data across environments. To address this challenge, organizations can use a storage abstraction layer like Portworx or Rook, which provide a consistent storage layer across multiple clouds and on-premise environments.

Resource Management: Managing resources across multiple clouds and on-premise environments can be challenging due to the differences in resource types and configurations. One solution to this challenge is to use a cloud management platform like Kubernetes Cluster API, which provides a consistent API for managing resources across multiple clouds and on-premise environments.

Security: Securing multi-cloud and hybrid cloud Kubernetes deployments is also a challenge due to the differences in security models and configurations. To address this challenge, organizations should adopt a unified security model that can be applied across multiple clouds and on-premise environments. This can include implementing mutual TLS authentication, encrypting data at rest and in transit, and implementing access controls and policies.

Monitoring and Management: Monitoring and managing multi-cloud and hybrid cloud Kubernetes deployments can be challenging due to the complexity of the environment. One best practice is to use a centralized management and monitoring tool like Rancher, which provides a unified dashboard for managing multiple clusters across different clouds and on-premise environments. Additionally, implementing observability tools like Prometheus and Grafana can help organizations monitor the performance and health of their Kubernetes clusters across multiple clouds and on-premise environments.

In summary, implementing multi-cloud and hybrid cloud Kubernetes deployments can be challenging due to the complexity of managing resources across multiple clouds and on-premise environments. However, by adopting best practices like using a service mesh, storage abstraction layer, cloud management platform, unified security model, and centralized monitoring and management tool, organizations can overcome these challenges and achieve a seamless, scalable, and secure Kubernetes deployment across multiple clouds and on-premise environments.

6.10 Explain the process of setting up and managing Kubernetes clusters on edge devices and IoT environments, and discuss the challenges and benefits of edge computing with Kubernetes.

Kubernetes is a popular container orchestration platform that is not only used in cloud environments but also in edge devices and IoT environments. Edge computing with Kubernetes involves setting up and managing Kubernetes clusters on devices that are located closer to the end-users, such as IoT devices, gateways, and edge servers. Here are some of the key steps and challenges in setting up and managing Kubernetes clusters on edge devices and IoT environments:

Hardware and Software Requirements: One of the first steps in setting up Kubernetes clusters on edge devices is to identify the hardware and software requirements. Since edge devices have limited resources and may not have a reliable network connection, it is important to choose the right hardware and software that can run Kubernetes efficiently. For example, organizations may choose to use lightweight Linux distributions like Alpine Linux or CoreOS, and edge-specific Kubernetes distributions like K3s or MicroK8s, which are designed to run on resource-constrained devices.

Edge-specific Use Cases: Another important consideration in setting up Kubernetes clusters on edge devices is to identify the edge-specific use cases and requirements. Edge computing with Kubernetes can be used for a wide range of use cases, such as real-time data processing, edge analytics, and edge AI/ML. Organizations need to identify the use cases that are relevant to their business and set up the Kubernetes clusters accordingly.

Network Connectivity: Since edge devices are typically located in remote or harsh environments, network connectivity can be a challenge. Organizations need to ensure that the Kubernetes clusters can operate even in low-bandwidth or intermittent network conditions. This may involve setting up edge-to-cloud connectivity using technologies like VPN or edge gateways.

Security: Securing Kubernetes clusters on edge devices is also a critical consideration. Since edge devices are located outside the traditional network perimeter, they are more vulnerable to attacks. Organizations need to implement security measures like encryption, access controls, and firewalls to ensure that the Kubernetes clusters are secure.

Monitoring and Management: Finally, organizations need to have a monitoring and management strategy in place for their Kubernetes clusters on edge devices. This involves monitoring the performance and health of the clusters, as well as managing software updates and patches. Organizations may choose to use edge-specific monitoring and management tools like Balena or OpenFaaS, which are designed for edge computing environments.

Benefits of Edge Computing with Kubernetes:

Edge computing with Kubernetes offers several benefits, such as:

Low Latency: Since edge devices are located closer to the end-users, edge computing with Kubernetes can offer lower latency and faster response times, which is critical for real-time applications.

Offline Operation: Kubernetes clusters on edge devices can operate even in offline or intermittent network conditions, which is important for remote or harsh environments.

Scalability: Edge computing with Kubernetes can also offer scalability, as organizations can easily add or remove edge devices to the Kubernetes cluster as needed.

Challenges of Edge Computing with Kubernetes:

Despite its benefits, edge computing with Kubernetes also poses several challenges, such as:

Resource Constraints: Edge devices typically have limited resources, which can make it challenging to run Kubernetes efficiently.

Security: Securing Kubernetes clusters on edge devices is also a challenge, as edge devices are more vulnerable to attacks.

Management Complexity: Managing Kubernetes clusters on edge devices can be complex, as organizations need to ensure that the clusters are updated, patched, and monitored regularly.

In summary, edge computing with Kubernetes involves setting up and managing Kubernetes clusters on edge devices and IoT environments. While it offers several benefits like low latency, offline operation, and scalability, it also poses challenges like resource constraints, security, and management complexity. By following best practices and using edge-specific Kubernetes distributions and tools, organizations can overcome these challenges and achieve a seamless, scalable, and secure Kubernetes deployment on edge devices and IoT environments

6.11 Describe the role of Custom Resource Definitions (CRDs) and their controllers in implementing domain-specific extensions to Kubernetes.

Custom Resource Definitions (CRDs) allow users to create custom resources in Kubernetes, extending the Kubernetes API with custom objects that represent applications, services, and other resources specific to their domain. This enables users to define and manage their applications and services in a more declarative and Kubernetes-native way, without having to rely on external tools and services.

CRDs are created using Kubernetes' API extension mechanism, which allows users to add new APIs to the Kubernetes API server. A CRD defines the structure and validation rules for the custom resource, including its metadata, schema, and status fields. Once a CRD is defined, users can create and manage instances of the custom resource using the Kubernetes API, kubectl, or client libraries.

CRDs are typically managed by custom controllers, which watch the Kubernetes API server for changes to the custom resource and perform operations based on the desired state of the resource. For example, a controller for a custom application resource might create and manage Pods, Services, and other Kubernetes objects to ensure the application is running as desired.

Custom controllers can be developed using various tools and frameworks, such as the Kubernetes Operator SDK, Kubebuilder, or plain Go code. These frameworks provide scaffolding and best practices for building controllers, including code generation, testing, and debugging tools.

Some popular examples of CRDs and their controllers include the Istio service mesh, which uses CRDs to define and manage virtual services, gateways, and other network resources, and the Prometheus monitoring system, which uses CRDs to define and manage alerting rules, recording rules, and other monitoring resources.

CRDs can be used to extend Kubernetes with custom functionality that is specific to an organization or domain, making it easier to manage complex applications and services in a Kubernetes-native way. However, it's important to follow best practices for developing and deploying custom resources and controllers, including proper validation, testing, and versioning.

6.12 How do you implement GitOps workflows in a Kubernetes environment, including versioning, rollbacks, and integration with CI/CD pipelines?

GitOps is an approach to managing Kubernetes infrastructure and application deployments that leverages version control systems (VCS) like Git for declarative configuration and deployment workflows. In a GitOps workflow, changes to the Kubernetes cluster or application configuration are made via Git commits, and are automatically applied to the cluster using continuous integration and continuous deployment (CI/CD) pipelines.

The GitOps workflow typically follows these steps:

Infrastructure and application configurations are defined in Git repositories, using Kubernetes manifests and other configuration files.

The Git repository is connected to a CI/CD pipeline, such as Jenkins, GitLab CI, or CircleCI.

The CI/CD pipeline monitors the Git repository for changes, and when changes are detected, it checks out the latest version of the code and applies it to the Kubernetes cluster using tools like kubectl, Helm, or other configuration management tools.

The changes are validated by running tests and automated checks against the cluster, and if they pass, the changes are committed back to Git with a version tag.

Rollbacks can be easily accomplished by reverting to a previous version of the configuration in Git, which is then automatically applied to the cluster.

Some benefits of using GitOps in a Kubernetes environment include improved version control, better auditability and traceability, and the ability to quickly roll back changes in case of errors or failures. Additionally, GitOps allows teams to manage multiple environments (such as development, staging, and production) with a single set of configuration files, which reduces the risk of configuration drift and improves consistency across environments.

To implement GitOps in a Kubernetes environment, there are several tools and frameworks available. Some popular ones include:

Flux: an open source GitOps operator for Kubernetes that can automatically sync Git repositories with Kubernetes clusters, and supports automated rollouts, rollbacks, and multi-tenancy.

Argo CD: a GitOps continuous delivery tool for Kubernetes that automates deployment of applications to multiple clusters, supports multiple Git repositories, and provides a web UI for managing deployments and rollbacks.

Jenkins X: a cloud-native CI/CD platform for Kubernetes that supports GitOps workflows, including automatic versioning, rollbacks, and integrations with Git hosting providers like GitHub and GitLab.

Implementing GitOps in a Kubernetes environment requires careful planning and design, including defining the desired state of the cluster, organizing configuration files into repositories and directories, and defining CI/CD pipelines and workflows that can handle rollouts, rollbacks, and versioning. It's also important to follow best practices for security, including using Git authentication and access controls to protect sensitive information in configuration files.

6.13 Discuss the process of container runtime interface (CRI) implementation in Kubernetes and compare different container runtime options.

In Kubernetes, the container runtime interface (CRI) defines the API between the Kubernetes kubelet and the container runtime responsible for running containers. The CRI was introduced to provide a standard interface for integrating different container runtimes with Kubernetes, allowing users to choose the runtime that best suits their needs.

The CRI consists of two main components: the runtime API and the image API. The runtime API defines the methods for managing the lifecycle of containers, including starting, stopping, and querying their status. The image API defines the methods for managing container images, including pulling, pushing, and listing images.

To implement the CRI in Kubernetes, a container runtime must provide a compatible implementation of the CRI API. Some of the popular container runtimes that support the CRI include Docker, containerd, and CRI-O.

Docker is the most widely used container runtime with Kubernetes, and it supports the CRI through a shim called "containerd". containerd is a daemon that manages the container lifecycle and image management on behalf of Docker. When a pod is created in Kubernetes, the kubelet sends a request to containerd to start the container, and containerd manages the container lifecycle from that point onwards.

CRI-O is a lightweight container runtime designed specifically for Kubernetes. It implements the CRI API natively and provides a more streamlined and efficient runtime compared to Docker. CRI-O supports a range of container image formats, including OCI and Docker, and provides features like live migration, automatic image garbage collection, and sandboxed container execution.

Another popular option for running containers in Kubernetes is containerd. Like CRI-O, containerd is a lightweight container runtime that implements the CRI API natively. containerd provides a simpler and more modular architecture compared to Docker, making it easier to maintain and customize. It also provides advanced features like checkpoint and restore, which allow containers to be paused and resumed at a later time.

In summary, the CRI plays a crucial role in allowing Kubernetes to integrate with different container runtimes. It provides a standard interface for managing containers and images, which enables users to choose the runtime that best fits their requirements. The most popular container runtimes that support the CRI include Docker, containerd, and CRI-O. Each of these runtimes has its strengths and weaknesses, and users should carefully evaluate their options before making a choice.

6.14 Explain the role of Kubernetes Admission Webhooks, their types (Validating and Mutating), and how they can be used to implement custom validation and mutation logic.

Kubernetes Admission Webhooks are a mechanism for intercepting requests to the Kubernetes API server before they are persisted to etcd. Admission Webhooks can be used to apply custom validation and mutation logic to Kubernetes resources, ensuring that only valid resources are deployed to the cluster. Admission Webhooks can be divided into two types: Validating and Mutating.

Validating Admission Webhooks intercept requests to the Kubernetes API server and can either accept or reject the request based on whether the request passes a set of validation rules. This can be useful for enforcing business policies or ensuring that certain security constraints are met. For example, a Validating Admission Webhook could be used to ensure that all Kubernetes resources contain a specific label or annotation, or to check that a user is authorized to make a particular request.

Mutating Admission Webhooks, on the other hand, can modify the request before it is persisted to etcd. This can be useful for applying default values or performing transformations on the request. For example, a Mutating Admission Webhook could be used to automatically add a label or annotation to all Kubernetes resources, or to convert a request from one API version to another.

To implement a custom Admission Webhook, you need to create a web service that receives requests from the Kubernetes API server. The web service should implement the appropriate Validating or Mutating Admission Webhook interface, which defines the methods for validating or mutating the request. The web service should also expose an HTTPS endpoint with a signed certificate that can be trusted by the Kubernetes API server.

Once the web service is deployed, you can register it with the Kubernetes API server by creating a ValidatingWebhookConfiguration or MutatingWebhookConfiguration object. These objects define the endpoint of the web service and the resources and operations that the Admission Webhook should intercept. When the Kubernetes API server receives a request that matches the configuration, it sends the request to the Admission Webhook for validation or mutation.

In conclusion, Admission Webhooks provide a powerful mechanism for customizing the behavior of the Kubernetes API server. They can be used to implement custom validation and mutation logic, enforce business policies, or apply default values and transformations to Kubernetes resources.

6.15 Describe advanced networking concepts in Kubernetes, such as network policies, ingress controllers, and service meshes, and discuss their impact on cluster performance and security.

Kubernetes is a powerful platform for managing containerized workloads at scale, and networking is a crucial aspect of its architecture. In this answer, we will discuss some advanced networking concepts in Kubernetes and their impact on cluster performance and security.

Network Policies

Network Policies are a Kubernetes feature that allows you to control the network traffic between pods in a cluster. By default, all pods can communicate with each other within a cluster, but Network Policies allow you to restrict this communication based on rules that you define. This can help you to enforce security policies and prevent unauthorized access to your network.

A Network Policy consists of a set of rules that define what traffic is allowed or denied between pods. The rules can be based on various criteria, such as the source or destination pod, the protocol used, and the port numbers. When a Network Policy is applied to a namespace, all pods in that namespace are subject to its rules.

Network Policies are implemented by a network plugin, and different plugins may have different capabilities. The most commonly used plugins are Calico, Cilium, and Weave Net.

Ingress Controllers

Ingress Controllers are another networking concept in Kubernetes that allows you to expose services to the outside world. An Ingress Controller is a Kubernetes resource that acts as a reverse proxy and routes incoming traffic to the appropriate services based on the URL path or hostname.

Ingress Controllers typically work with an Ingress Resource, which is a Kubernetes object that defines the routing rules for incoming traffic. An Ingress Resource can be used to configure SSL/TLS termination, load balancing, and other advanced features.

There are several Ingress Controllers available for Kubernetes, including Nginx, Traefik, and Istio. Each Ingress Controller has its own set of features and capabilities, so it's important to choose one that best suits your needs.

Service Meshes

Service Meshes are a newer concept in Kubernetes that aims to solve some of the challenges of microservices networking. A Service Mesh is a dedicated infrastructure layer for managing service-to-service communication within a cluster.

Service Meshes typically use a sidecar proxy model, where each pod has an additional container that acts as a proxy for all incoming and outgoing traffic. The proxy intercepts all traffic and can perform various tasks, such as load balancing, service discovery, and encryption.

The two most popular Service Meshes for Kubernetes are Istio and Linkerd. These Service Meshes offer advanced features such as traffic management, observability, and security, but they also introduce additional complexity to the networking layer.

In conclusion, advanced networking concepts such as Network Policies, Ingress Controllers, and Service Meshes play a crucial role in Kubernetes deployments. They offer powerful features for controlling and securing network traffic, but they also require careful consideration and planning to ensure optimal performance and security.

6.16   Discuss strategies for implementing and enforcing compliance and governance policies in a Kubernetes environment, including cluster hardening, policy engines, and auditing.

Kubernetes is a powerful platform for deploying and managing containerized applications. However, with great power comes great responsibility, and it's important to ensure that Kubernetes environments comply with regulatory and governance policies. In this context, compliance and governance refer to a set of rules and policies that organizations must follow to meet legal, regulatory, and business requirements.

Here are some strategies for implementing and enforcing compliance and governance policies in a Kubernetes environment:

Cluster Hardening: One of the first steps in securing a Kubernetes cluster is to harden it by limiting access, applying security patches, and configuring secure network policies. Hardening a Kubernetes cluster involves disabling unnecessary APIs and using network policies to restrict traffic between pods.

Policy Engines: Kubernetes has a built-in policy framework called "Open Policy Agent" (OPA), which allows organizations to define policies that govern the behavior of their Kubernetes clusters. Policies can be enforced at various levels, such as namespaces, deployments, and Pods. OPA provides a declarative language called Rego, which makes it easy to define policies in a human-readable format.

Auditing: Kubernetes provides auditing capabilities that allow organizations to track the activity of users and resources within the cluster. Auditing logs can be stored in a centralized location for analysis and reporting. Kubernetes also provides tools for analyzing and visualizing audit logs, such as Kibana and Elasticsearch.

Compliance Testing: Kubernetes provides a tool called "Sonobuoy" that helps to ensure that a Kubernetes cluster is configured according to best practices and compliance policies. Sonobuoy runs a set of tests against a Kubernetes cluster and generates a report that indicates whether the cluster is compliant or not.

Role-Based Access Control (RBAC): RBAC allows organizations to control access to Kubernetes resources based on the role of the user or group. RBAC can be used to restrict access to sensitive resources, such as secrets, and ensure that only authorized users can modify critical resources.

Image Scanning: Container images that are deployed in a Kubernetes cluster should be scanned for vulnerabilities before they are used. Image scanning tools, such as Aqua Security and Trivy, can scan images for known vulnerabilities and provide a report that can be used to determine whether the image is compliant or not.

Continuous Compliance: Compliance policies and rules are not static and may change over time. Organizations should implement a continuous compliance strategy that ensures that their Kubernetes environment is always compliant. This involves setting up automated compliance checks, monitoring compliance status, and making necessary changes to maintain compliance.

In summary, Kubernetes provides several tools and capabilities that can be used to enforce compliance and governance policies in a Kubernetes environment. Organizations should implement a combination of these strategies to ensure that their Kubernetes environment is secure, compliant, and governed.

6.17 Explain the process of integrating Kubernetes with external storage systems and databases, considering factors like data consistency, latency, and backup/restore strategies.

Kubernetes provides various options to integrate with external storage systems and databases. This integration is crucial as it helps in providing persistent storage to stateful applications running on Kubernetes. Some of the popular storage systems and databases that can be integrated with Kubernetes include Amazon EBS, Google Cloud Persistent Disks, NFS, Ceph, GlusterFS, and more.

Kubernetes provides two primary methods for integrating with external storage systems: dynamic provisioning and static provisioning.

Dynamic Provisioning: In this method, Kubernetes automatically provisions storage volumes as needed. This method is preferred over static provisioning because it avoids the need to pre-allocate storage resources, and it can scale automatically as the application workload changes. Kubernetes uses Storage Classes to define the different types of storage that can be dynamically provisioned. A Storage Class is defined as a set of parameters that describe the storage system to use, the access mode, and other parameters that determine how the storage should be provisioned.

Static Provisioning: In this method, the storage resources are pre-allocated and then mounted to the Pods that need them. This method is useful when you have specific storage requirements that cannot be met by dynamic provisioning.

To integrate with external databases, Kubernetes provides StatefulSets, which are used to manage stateful applications running on Kubernetes. A StatefulSet creates and manages a set of identical Pods with unique network identities that are attached to stable storage. Each Pod in a StatefulSet is assigned a unique hostname and a unique persistent identifier that is based on the Pod's ordinal index in the set. This ensures that each Pod has a stable network identity that can be used to connect to external databases.

To ensure data consistency, Kubernetes provides Volume Snapshots that can be used to backup and restore data from persistent volumes. Volume Snapshots can be used to create point-in-time backups of persistent volumes, and these backups can be used to restore the data in the event of a disaster or data corruption.

Overall, integrating Kubernetes with external storage systems and databases is essential to ensure that stateful applications can run reliably and at scale on Kubernetes. By using dynamic provisioning, static provisioning, StatefulSets, and Volume Snapshots, you can ensure that your applications have access to the storage resources they need and that data is protected and backed up appropriately.

6.18 How do you manage cluster upgrades and versioning in a Kubernetes environment, including best practices for minimizing downtime and ensuring backward compatibility?

Managing cluster upgrades and versioning is a crucial aspect of maintaining a healthy Kubernetes environment. Upgrading to newer versions of Kubernetes is essential to take advantage of new features, security patches, and bug fixes. However, the upgrade process can be challenging, as it involves upgrading the control plane and worker nodes while minimizing downtime.

Here are some strategies for managing cluster upgrades and versioning in a Kubernetes environment:

Plan the upgrade: Before upgrading a Kubernetes cluster, it is essential to plan the upgrade carefully. Identify the current version of Kubernetes running in the cluster and the target version to which the cluster needs to be upgraded. Check the release notes of the target version and identify any breaking changes, new features, or deprecations that need to be addressed. Plan the upgrade process and identify the order in which the control plane and worker nodes need to be upgraded.

Upgrade the control plane: Upgrading the control plane is the first step in the upgrade process. It involves upgrading the API server, etcd, and controller manager components. The control plane upgrade can be done using tools like kubeadm or the Kubernetes cluster API. During the upgrade process, it is important to keep the control plane running and minimize downtime.

Upgrade the worker nodes: Once the control plane is upgraded, the worker nodes can be upgraded. This involves upgrading the kubelet, kube-proxy, and other node-specific components. The upgrade process can be done using tools like kubeadm or node refresh. During the upgrade process, the worker nodes need to be drained, and the Pods need to be rescheduled to other nodes to avoid downtime.

Test the upgraded cluster: Once the upgrade process is complete, it is important to test the upgraded cluster to ensure that it is functioning correctly. Run end-to-end tests and validate the functionality of the applications running on the cluster. If any issues are identified, they need to be addressed before the cluster is made available for production use.

Maintain backward compatibility: It is essential to ensure that the upgraded cluster is backward compatible with the existing applications running on the cluster. The upgraded cluster should support the existing APIs and features, and the applications should continue to function as expected. If any breaking changes are identified, they need to be addressed before the cluster is made available for production use.

In addition to the above strategies, it is also essential to ensure that the Kubernetes environment is regularly updated with security patches and bug fixes. Regular upgrades and maintenance help ensure that the Kubernetes environment is secure, stable, and up-to-date with the latest features and capabilities.

6.19 Discuss the role of machine learning and artificial intelligence in optimizing Kubernetes cluster management, including workload placement, autoscaling, and anomaly detection.

Machine learning (ML) and artificial intelligence (AI) technologies are becoming increasingly important in managing Kubernetes clusters, as they can help optimize various aspects of cluster operations, such as resource allocation, workload placement, and autoscaling.

In this response, we will discuss some of the ways ML and AI are being used in Kubernetes management, as well as some examples of tools and technologies that are available for these purposes.

One of the primary ways ML and AI are being used in Kubernetes management is through the use of predictive analytics. Predictive analytics involves using statistical models and machine learning algorithms to analyze large amounts of data and make predictions about future events or behaviors. In the context of Kubernetes, predictive analytics can be used to identify patterns in workload behavior and resource usage, and to make predictions about how workloads will behave under different conditions.

For example, the Kubernetes Horizontal Pod Autoscaler (HPA) uses predictive analytics to determine when to scale up or down the number of replicas for a particular workload. The HPA analyzes the resource usage of the workload over time and makes predictions about how much additional capacity will be needed to handle future demand. This allows the cluster to scale up or down proactively, rather than waiting until demand has already exceeded capacity.

Another area where ML and AI are being used in Kubernetes management is in workload placement. Kubernetes provides several mechanisms for specifying placement constraints, such as node affinity/anti-affinity rules and pod topology spread constraints. ML algorithms can be used to optimize these placement decisions, taking into account factors such as resource utilization, network latency, and data locality.

For example, the Kubernetes scheduler can be extended to use custom scheduling algorithms that incorporate ML and AI techniques. The OpenAI Gym-Kubernetes project provides a gym-like environment for developing and testing custom scheduling algorithms, using reinforcement learning and other ML techniques.

Finally, ML and AI can be used in Kubernetes management for anomaly detection and proactive remediation. ML algorithms can be used to analyze metrics and logs from the cluster and detect abnormal patterns of behavior or resource usage. When anomalies are detected, automated remediation actions can be triggered, such as scaling up resources or restarting pods.

There are several tools and technologies available for incorporating ML and AI into Kubernetes management. For example, the Kubernetes Metrics Server provides a scalable way to collect resource utilization data from pods and nodes, which can be used as input to ML algorithms. The Prometheus monitoring system provides a powerful platform for collecting and analyzing time-series data from Kubernetes clusters, and can be used to build custom anomaly detection and alerting workflows.

In summary, ML and AI are increasingly important in managing Kubernetes clusters, as they can help optimize various aspects of cluster operations and improve the efficiency and resiliency of the cluster. There are several tools and technologies available for incorporating ML and AI into Kubernetes management, and we can expect to see continued innovation in this area in the coming years.

6.20 Describe the challenges and opportunities in the evolution of the Kubernetes ecosystem, including emerging technologies, open-source projects, and community-driven initiatives.

Kubernetes has rapidly become the standard for container orchestration and has a thriving ecosystem that is constantly evolving. Some of the challenges and opportunities in the evolution of the Kubernetes ecosystem include:

Complexity: As Kubernetes has grown in popularity, it has become more complex to manage and operate. This has led to the emergence of tools and frameworks that simplify the deployment and management of Kubernetes clusters, such as Kubespray, Kubeadm, and Rancher.

Multicloud support: Kubernetes has become a popular choice for multicloud deployments, allowing organizations to deploy and manage workloads across multiple cloud providers. This has led to the emergence of cloud-specific managed Kubernetes offerings, such as Amazon EKS, Google GKE, and Microsoft AKS.

Security: Kubernetes has a rich set of security features, including role-based access control (RBAC), network policies, and pod security policies. However, the increasing complexity of Kubernetes clusters and the rise of security threats has made security a top concern for organizations.

Service mesh integration: As microservices architectures become more prevalent, the need for service meshes has grown. Service meshes provide features such as traffic management, security, and observability for microservices. Kubernetes has integrated with service mesh solutions like Istio, Linkerd, and Consul to provide these features.

Serverless computing: Kubernetes has been adapted for serverless computing through the Knative project, which provides a platform for building, deploying, and managing serverless workloads on Kubernetes.

AI and machine learning: Kubernetes has become a platform for running machine learning workloads, with frameworks like Kubeflow providing a set of tools for building and deploying machine learning models on Kubernetes clusters.

Community-driven innovation: The Kubernetes community is vibrant and constantly evolving, with contributions from a diverse set of individuals and organizations. This has led to the emergence of new projects and initiatives, such as the Kubernetes Operators project and the Cloud Native Computing Foundation (CNCF).

Overall, the evolution of the Kubernetes ecosystem presents both challenges and opportunities for organizations. By embracing the latest technologies and best practices, organizations can take full advantage of the power and flexibility of Kubernetes to build and deploy modern, scalable, and secure applications.

Made in the USA
Monee, IL
08 January 2025